WIDE EYED EDITIONS

CONTENTS

WHEN YOU'RE FEELING
SAD, HEARTBROKEN, BLUE,
OR LOST,

CRY IT OUT WITH...

LANA DEL REY
BORN: June 21, 1985
HOMETOWN: Lake Placid, New York
ALBUMS SOLD: 30 million
AWARDS WON: 2 BRIT Awards

CRY IT OUT WITH

Lana Del Rey

TO UNDERSTAND LANA DEL REY, YOU HAVE TO LISTEN TO HER BIGGEST SONG TO DATE, "SUMMERTIME SADNESS." IT'S A SONG ABOUT SAYING GOODBYE TO A LOVED ONE, WHICH IS SOMETHING A LOT OF PEOPLE CAN IDENTIFY WITH.

But the unique thing about Lana Del Rey is that she's able to take her emotions and blow them up into fireworks. "Summertime Sadness" is a big, epic ballad that makes life seem pretty dazzling even in its saddest moments. Being sad is hard, but songs like Lana Del Rey's make you remember feeling down is okay—even when it's sunny out!—and that it can lead to big breakthroughs. On early songs like "YOUNG AND BEAUTIFUL" and "VIDEO GAMES," she captures this too, never being shy of big feelings. In her music videos—big, glitzy productions that seem fantastical—she captures all the beauty and the glory of being sad.

Most of her songs are super slow, very sad songs about love and fame. Sometimes music can help you understand yourself, and other times, it will take you places you've never been before. Listening to Lana Del Rey songs can make you feel like you're the star of a black-and-white movie where everything has gone wrong. Sometimes that's just the music you need to hear to make you feel like your problems aren't so wild after all.

Still, Lana knows that life isn't all bad. On her 2017 album *Lust for Life*, she had a much rosier view of the world, especially on its first single "LOVE." It's all about being young and in love, with lots of soaring strings that make your heart jump out of your chest. As the singer told her idol Stevie Nicks in an interview that year, "Love makes the world go 'round." Even the saddest artists in the world recognize the power of love, and that's why she chose to put "Love" before any other songs on the album.

CRY IT OUT WITH

AMY WINEHOUSE

AMY WINEHOUSE'S STORY IS ONE OF THE SADDEST STORIES IN MUSIC HISTORY.

The British singer made some of the most creative music ever recorded. On her two albums, *Frank* and *Back to Black*, she blended old-school soul sounds with modern R&B and hip-hop influences. Her music told sad stories about toxic people and bad relationships, but in a very beautiful way. On "TEARS DRY ON THEIR OWN," she takes one of the most treasured love songs of all time, "AIN'T NO MOUNTAIN HIGH ENOUGH," and twists it into her own dark creation that makes you dance and cry at the same time. You might also love her cover of "VALERIE," a love song that sounds like it could be from any decade—from the 1950s to now. There's really nothing else like it.

Unfortunately, Amy's real life was too tough to handle and she died at 27, after struggling with substance abuse for a long time. She talked about those problems in her most well-known song, "REHAB." It's so easy to sing along and dance to that you might forget that it's actually about a very sad story. That song's lyrics, which talked about people begging her to seek treatment for her problems, was her real life story.

Amy's dad Mitch probably best explained why her songs shake people up so much: "It was precisely because her songs were dragged up out of her soul that they were so powerful and passionate," he wrote in a book about her life. "The ones that went into *Back to Black* were about the deepest emotions."

Amy's story is a lesson that we should always be willing to accept help when we need it. It's also a lesson to keep good people around you no matter what. To get through your darkest time, it always helps to have people who will look out for you.

AMY WINEHOUSE
BORN: September 14, 1983
HOMETOWN: London, England
BONUS FACT: Amy's signature beehive hairdo was a tribute to 60s girl groups.
AWARDS WON: 6 Grammy Awards

JAMES BLAKE

JAMES BLAKE
BORN: September 26, 1988
HOMETOWN: London, England
ESSENTIAL ALBUM: Overgrown
AWARDS WON: 1 Grammy; the Mercury Prize

SOMETIMES SADNESS MAKES US FEEL STUCK; IT'S HARD TO BE PRODUCTIVE WHEN YOU DON'T FEEL GREAT. BUT UK MUSICIAN JAMES BLAKE'S ART IS A REMINDER THAT SADNESS CAN BE USED AS A TOOL TO DO GREAT THINGS.

Speaking to *The Fader* in 2011, he told the story of how a breakup in high school inspired the way he made some of his early music. "Maybe it's a good thing that that happened," he recalled, "because now I can write some really good music. Not just silver lining, but I'm glad that happened, even in the moment, because now I can write something really charged." He took a negative situation and found the most positive outcome in it.

Blake uses that same superpower—the ability to find the beauty in sadness—to help other people unlock their emotions too. He mainly makes electronic and piano music in his solo work, but he's found great success as a collaborator with rappers and big pop musicians, like Travis Scott, Jay-Z, and Beyoncé. In those collaborations, you can almost feel his sadness creep into the other artists' voices.

For a taste of just how powerful Blake can be with his raw emotions, listen to "RETROGRADE." The beginning of the song showcases his floaty voice alongside little claps and some tender piano. At the song's climax, apocalyptic digital horns break up the sad party. It makes you feel a little nuts but in a good way. By the time the song ends, those noises have been chased out by Blake's gentle singing. It's a reminder for listeners that strong feelings come and go, that eventually the storm will pass and hopefully you'll be left with a rainbow at the other end. Blake got his own little rainbow with his 2019 album *Assume Form*, a collection of songs all about finding love.

CRY IT OUT WITH

KACEY MUSGRAVES

KACEY MUSGRAVES
BORN: August 21, 1988
HOMETOWN: Golden,
Texas, USA
BONUS FACT: Her
grandma cried when she
found out that Kacey
pierced her nose.
AWARDS WON: 6
Grammy Awards;
5 Country Music
Association Awards

KACEY MUSGRAVES MAKES MUSIC ABOUT MEMORIES. SHE MAKES COUNTRY MUSIC THAT IS FOR EVERYBODY, BUT ESPECIALLY PEOPLE WHO KNOW WHAT IT'S LIKE TO LIVE IN SMALL TOWNS OR HAVE BIG DREAMS.

On her first album, *Same Trailer Different Park*, she told the world what life was like in her small hometown of Golden, Texas. It turns out life there was just as deep as it is in any big city, filled with colorful characters and lots of ambition inside her mind. It's the kind of album that can make you feel sad about missing a place you haven't even left yet. Later, she penned the song "FAMILY IS FAMILY," all about how special your family is, no matter what kind of people are in it or what it looks like. She's not the typical country star, and she's sung a lot about what it's like to not fit in. Listen to "FOLLOW YOUR ARROW," "PAGEANT MATERIAL," and "BISCUITS" if you want to get inspired about charting your own course. She writes about a lot of different subjects, but she always makes you feel something.

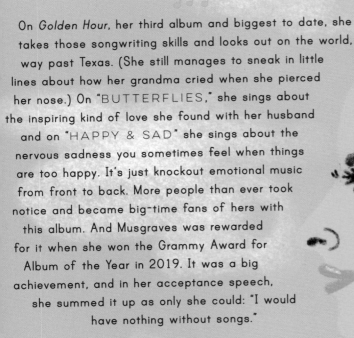

On *Golden Hour*, her third album and biggest to date, she takes those songwriting skills and looks out on the world, way past Texas. (She still manages to sneak in little lines about how her grandma cried when she pierced her nose.) On "BUTTERFLIES," she sings about the inspiring kind of love she found with her husband and on "HAPPY & SAD" she sings about the nervous sadness you sometimes feel when things are too happy. It's just knockout emotional music from front to back. More people than ever took notice and became big-time fans of hers with this album. And Musgraves was rewarded for it when she won the Grammy Award for Album of the Year in 2019. It was a big achievement, and in her acceptance speech, she summed it up as only she could: "I would have nothing without songs."

CRY IT OUT WITH

ZAYN

SOMETIMES WHEN YOU HAVE A FAVORITE BAND, THEY DON'T STAY TOGETHER. LIKE ALL PARTNERSHIPS AND FRIENDSHIPS, SOMETIMES THINGS CHANGE.

There once was a group called One Direction. The original line-up was made up of five guys from the UK: Niall Horan, Liam Payne, Harry Styles, Louis Tomlinson, and Zayn Malik. They had lots of success and had an army of fans who loved them very much. For a taste of what made them great, listen to the phenomenal "STORY OF MY LIFE." It might make you shed a tear or two. But in 2015, things changed when Zayn left the group to make music by himself. At first, some fans were very upset and were even brought to tears over it. But soon, they understood why he left and accepted his changes.

But Zayn went off on his own and made great music as a solo artist. He sings a lot about love and relationships. And while it's not the same music he became famous for, it's just different and really good. He's still great at collaborating with others too. For proof of that, listen to "I DON'T WANNA LIVE FOREVER," his song with Taylor Swift. His voice is stunning. A couple of years after Zayn left the band, they all went on to have solo careers of their own. Now there's lots of music from the boys to enjoy. It's a reminder that an upsetting situation can turn into something that's just as amazing.

Zayn simply didn't want the same kind of fame that the band had. "By the time I decided to go," he said later that year to *The Fader*, "it just felt right on that day. I woke up on that morning, and was like, 'I need to go home. I just need to be me now, because I've had enough.'" Speaking up for yourself is always important.

ZAYN
BORN: January 12, 1993
HOMETOWN: Bradford, England
BONUS FACT: Zayn once built a
pirate-themed shed in his backyard.
AWARDS WON: 1 American Music
Award; 1 Billboard Music Award

CRY IT OUT WITH

Adele

SO, YOU'VE GOT A CRUSH ON SOMEONE... AND MAYBE THEY DON'T LIKE YOU BACK—OR EVEN KNOW YOU EXIST.

That might hurt pretty badly. For those kinds of moments, you might need to go into a really quiet place and listen to one of the UK's most powerful voices, Adele. If there's anyone in the world who understands what that feels like, it's her.

Adele released her first album, *19*, in 2008, and since then has taken over the whole world with her songs about the power of love. She's won just about every award you can think of because she's able to make people feel very powerful emotions with her voice. Fans from all over the world love to hear her sing about those sad times that everyone can relate to. Her song "SOMEONE LIKE YOU" is one of the best songs ever about having your heart broken. Listen for how her voice doesn't always sound perfectly sweet or steady—that edge is what makes her songs feel even more real and special.

Adele songs are also super fun to sing along to because she's such a great singer. You might not hit all the notes that she can, but it's still fun to try. Listen to her song "HELLO." It's a very epic song from her album *25*, where she's singing to someone she used to love. This might sound weird, but it sounds like getting stuck on top of a mountain with a big tornado blowing around you. See if you can hold out the notes for as long as she can—it's almost impossible.

It's all right to cry to Adele, or if you're having a bad day and don't end up shedding any tears, that's okay too. You might also try listening to "ROLLING IN THE DEEP," a boot-stomping song about getting even with someone who made you upset. Heartbreak isn't easy, but after some solo Adele karaoke, you'll be that much closer to getting back on your feet.

ADELE
BORN: May 5, 1988
HOMETOWN: London, England
ALBUMS SOLD: Over 40 million
AWARDS WON: 1 Academy Award; 9 BRIT Awards; 15 Grammy Awards

CRY IT OUT WITH

Joni Mitchell

JONI MITCHELL
BORN: November 7, 1943
HOMETOWN: Fort MacLeod,
Alberta, Canada
ESSENTIAL ALBUM: Blue
AWARDS WON: 9 Grammy
Awards; Induction into Rock and
Roll Hall of Fame

THERE ARE SOME SPECIAL ALBUMS THAT CAN REALLY MAKE YOU BREAK DOWN. FOR LOTS AND LOTS OF PEOPLE, THAT ALBUM IS *BLUE* BY JONI MITCHELL.

One of the greatest songwriters of all time, Mitchell got her start making original folk music in Canada. Eventually she reached the US and made lots of music—some very political—that helped define the 1970s as an era.

Her song "BIG YELLOW TAXI" is a perfect example of her graceful skillset: strumming guitars, meaningful lyrics, but most importantly, incredibly catchy melodies. The song has been covered by lots of people hoping to have Joni's magic rub off on them. On *Blue*, which came out in 1971, she released a collection of songs so personal it changed how people around the world thought about one another. From "MY OLD MAN" to "A CASE OF YOU," every song on the album is emotional enough to make someone cry. They're songs about her real-life relationships and what happened during them. It all just sounds so honest.

The album is an important one because it shows how powerful you can be when you show people your real emotions. You might think putting up a strong front all of the time makes you brave, but there's a different kind of muscle when you show and tell people what you're really going through. Letting down your defenses is a good thing and listening to Joni Mitchell can draw those things out of you.

As Mitchell explained to *Rolling Stone* at the end of her biggest decade, she let everything go when she wrote the album: "I felt like I had absolutely no secrets from the world and I couldn't pretend in my life to be strong," she said. "Or to be happy. But the advantage of it in the music was that there were no defenses there either."

JEFF BUCKLEY

IF THERE'S ONE SONG THAT CAN MAKE PEOPLE CRY, IT'S PROBABLY JEFF BUCKLEY'S "HALLELUJAH."

It's been featured in movies and TV shows, and you may have heard many different versions of it already. There's something about the melody and the mysterious lyrics that lets people project their feelings onto this bewitching piece of music. The song was originally written by Canadian singer Leonard Cohen in the 1980s. But the version that really shook the world was a cover by Jeff Buckley that kicked off many more attempts to master this special piece of music. Listen to his version. It starts off with twangy guitar and then Buckley's voice comes in, like a soft whisper, just barely noticeable around the twinkling instruments. But as he sings the song, his voice rises, and then falls back down again to whisper the song's title so softly it feels like he's crying. It'll stay in your heart forever.

Listening to Jeff Buckley makes you feel like someone has gone through your problems before and you can get out of it. The song definitely speaks to his intentions of making music. As he told an interviewer in 1995, "I don't really have a major message that I want to bring to the world through my music. The music can tell people everything they need to know about being human beings. It's not my information, it's not mine. I didn't make it. I just discovered it."

The song is just the beginning of what makes him so special as an artist. He only released one album in his lifetime, the stunning *Grace* in 1994. Yes, "HALLELUJAH" is its centerpiece, but tracks like "LAST GOODBYE" and "SO REAL" show that he has the range to excel in a lot of different modes. Tragically, he passed away in an accident before he could record more music, making that album and "Hallelujah" even more special. Even though his musical career was so brief, he's been included on several lists proclaiming that he has one of the best voices of all time.

JEFF BUCKLEY
BORN: November 17, 1966
HOMETOWN: Anaheim, California, USA
BONUS FACT: His first performance was in a church.
ESSENTIAL ALBUM: Grace

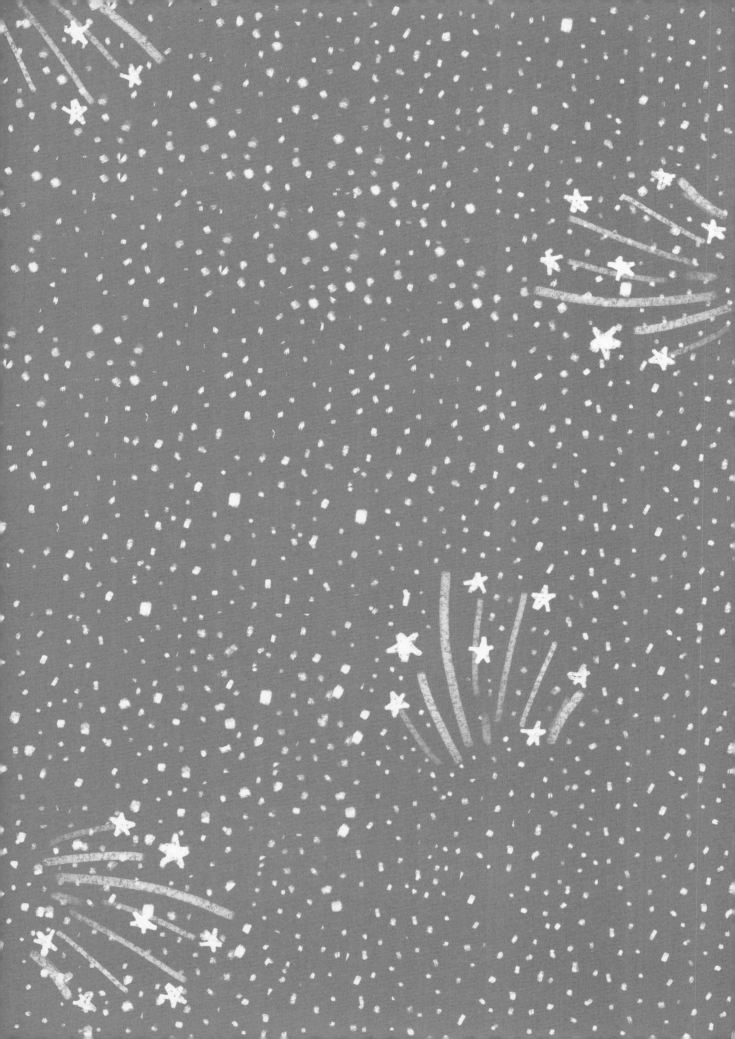

WHEN YOU ARE INSPIRED,
ENERGETIC, IMAGINATIVE,
OR EVEN BORED,

GET CREATIVE WITH...

MISSY ELLIOTT
BORN: JULY 1, 1971
HOMETOWN: Portsmouth, Virginia, USA
ALBUMS SOLD: 14 million
AWARDS WON: 5 Grammy Awards

GET CREATIVE WITH

MISSY ELLIOTT

TO UNDERSTAND JUST HOW CREATIVE MISSY ELLIOTT IS, YOU HAVE TO WATCH HER MUSIC VIDEOS.

Start with "THE RAIN (SUPA DUPA FLY)." It's the song that really introduced the world to just how delightfully inventive Missy is. There she is: with red glasses that turn into a gold crown, wearing a big black coat that looks like a garbage bag. A second later, she's wearing a yellow jacket that's as bright as a thousand lemons and wiggling her arms like they're going to fall off. But it's not just her fashion or dance moves that make Missy one of the most creative artists of all time: it's her music. "The Rain" is a freakishly awesome song. The beat in the background is what you might imagine aliens on Mars sound like. About a minute into the song, Missy's voice beeps like a car and then launches into a swaggering verse. She keeps her voice chill and repeats little syllables and it all sounds like it's being sung in a mystifying dream.

That song is just one example of how she constantly broke away from what was expected of her. Not only did she rap, she sang, too. She's also an amazing producer. Missy isn't afraid of using every crayon in the box and then using the empty box to make a new hat for herself.

As a little kid, Missy would lock herself in her room and stage performances, building her own little universe. At school, when her teachers would ask what she wanted to be, she set her goals as high as she could imagine.

"I would be like, 'I'm going to be a superstar!'" she revealed in a 2017 interview in ELLE magazine. "And the whole class would bust out laughing. But every Friday I would say the same thing. And I would watch them change to different things, but still, I wanted to be a superstar. They thought I was the class clown. But I was like, 'I'm going to be a superstar.' So when I would get in my room, it was like, if y'all don't see it, I'm going to create it myself."

GET CREATIVE WITH

Janet Jackson

JANET JACKSON
BORN: May 16, 1966
HOMETOWN: Gary, Indiana, USA
ESSENTIAL ALBUM: Control
AWARDS WON: 5 Grammy Awards

THERE COMES A TIME WHEN YOU HAVE TO TAKE CHARGE OF YOUR OWN LIFE, LOOK DEEP INSIDE YOURSELF, AND FIGURE OUT WHAT REALLY MATTERS TO YOU.

For artist Janet Jackson, that time came around 1986. The singer (and little sister of the very successful Jackson 5) had released two albums and seen a bit of success. But she was still in the shadow of her brothers and her music wasn't yet as fully appreciated as it is now.

Then came her album *Control*. In a 2018 *Billboard* magazine interview, she spoke on what it was like when she started making that album and unlocked her true creative process. "I knew I had something to say," she said. "I knew I had to assert myself. I also knew I had to go through the painful process of what my brothers had gone through. I had to thank my father for his help and then move on. I had to assert myself."

With the help of her producers and friends Jimmy Jam and Terry Lewis, she was able to tap into her most ambitious self and show the world all of her uniqueness. She created a whole new sound called "New Jack Swing." It was an update of R&B that borrowed some elements from hip-hop. It reinvented what people wanted to dance to. The album was eye-opening and people saw Janet in a whole new light.

Three years later, she released her masterpiece, *Rhythm Nation 1814*. It's a fearless album that makes you feel defiant and strong when you listen to it. Listen to the title track of that album—it will make you want to dance but you still hang on her every word. By believing in herself, and by trying to be as authentic as possible, Janet was able to make the most creative music of her career. It empowered people all over the world and extended way beyond herself.

GET CREATIVE WITH

PHARRELL WILLIAMS

PHARRELL WILLIAMS
BORN: April 5, 1973
HOMETOWN: Virginia Beach, Virginia, USA
ALBUMS SOLD: 3 million +
AWARDS WON: 13 Grammy Awards

WHEN YOU HEAR A SONG THAT WAS MADE BY PHARRELL WILLIAMS, YOU'LL KNOW IT RIGHT AWAY.

One clue is that most of his songs start the exact same way: you'll hear the same beat played four times in a row, like the record is skipping back and forth. Other keys to recognizing a Pharrell track? The drums. Pharrell is a master percussionist. He got his musical start playing snare drum in his high school marching band, and you can hear his talents on the drums in most of the songs he makes. Both of those are helpful, but there's another secret way to identify a Pharrell song— they're usually the catchiest songs you've ever heard.

Take, for example, "HAPPY." It starts off w that four-beat pattern. Then there's the drumming that immediately gets your feet tapping. The music feels old but new at the same time, and almost every part of the son gets stuck in your head. As soon as you hear those first few notes, you just can't help but smile—that's the magic of Pharrell. The track was the best-selling single of 2014 and spent 10 weeks at number one in the US charts. It was just the latest smash from the brain of a man who can turn anything into a hit.

For a lot of artists, Pharrell has always been able to crack the code of what makes a great song. He's made beats for rap songs, soulful R&B songs, and sugary pop masterpieces. No matter what, he's always up for a challenge. In fact, that's what he says keeps his music so creative and different in the first place.

"Comfort is very sneaky," he said in a 20 interview in Inc. magazine. "It feels good, and sometimes you don't even realize you're comfortable. But in order to get the best out of yourself, you have to put yourself into positions where you're uncomfortable or vulnerable."

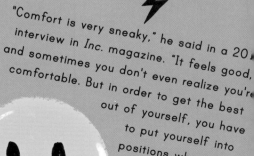

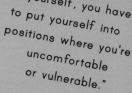

GET CREATIVE WITH

PRINCE

BORN: June 7, 1958
HOMETOWN: Minneapolis, Minnesota, USA
ALBUMS SOLD: 100 million +
AWARDS WON: 7 Grammy Awards;
1 Academy Award

PRINCE ALWAYS KEPT PEOPLE GUESSING. FROM HIS FIRST ALBUM IN 1978 TO HIS 39TH RELEASE IN 2015, THE SINGER AND POP MASTERMIND ALWAYS OFFERED UP SOMETHING NEW FOR HIS FANS.

Across his career, Prince drifted between rock, R&B, pop, soul, and more. Sometimes he offered up double albums, others were short deliveries. One time, he made an entire soundtrack for a Batman movie (it's spectacular). In the 1990s, Prince changed his name to a symbol that no one could pronounce. There was just no figuring him out and that's what everyone loved about him. "The most important thing is to be true to yourself, but I also like danger," he said in 1982 to the *LA Times*. "That's what's missing from pop music today. There's no excitement or mystery."

Prince's music was just as innovative as the way he approached the world. Listen to *Purple Rain*, the soundtrack to a film Prince starred in. The movie was loosely based on Prince's life and is a great canvas for showing off his gifts. Try listening to "LET'S GO CRAZY." From the organ and Prince's voiceover that start off the track, you just know it's going to be a moment. Then it breaks into a beat that's so insanely fun to dance to. Later there's a guitar solo that practically melts your ears off.

Prince was a master at guitar and is generally considered to be one of the best players of all time. What makes his guitar solos so special is that same sense of unpredictability. Sometimes they're wild, jumping all over the place. Other times, they're tightly controlled and like soft meditations. Whenever you hear a new Prince guitar part you haven't heard before, you can be sure that you're going to be surprised. There's a special sort of power that comes when people don't really understand what you're serving up to them. No one knew that better than Prince.

GET CREATIVE WITH

The Beatles

THE BEATLES
BORN: 1940–1943
HOMETOWN: Liverpool, United Kingdom
ALBUMS SOLD: 600 million
ESSENTIAL ALBUM: The White Album
AWARDS WON: 14 Grammy Awards;
1 Academy Award

SINCE 1962, ALL BANDS HAVE HAD TO STAND IN COMPARISON TO THE BEATLES. THAT'S THE YEAR "LOVE ME DO" TOOK OVER LONDON FIRST, AND THEN THE WHOLE WORLD.

Together, John Lennon, Paul McCartney, George Harrison, and Ringo Starr whipped up teenagers everywhere into a craze that was nicknamed "Beatlemania." Wherever they went, people screamed and lost their minds. At first, their music was playful and sweet. Listen to "I WANT TO HOLD YOUR HAND" to get a sense of what made them so popular. It's incredibly memorable and relatively simple, but at the time it was seen as pretty radical. The Beatles are generally given credit for making rock and roll as popular as it ever would be. Listening to their music made people dance and smile.

But any band could be well-liked. The Beatles were much more than that. What made them so influential is that, as they became more confident musicians, they became even bigger innovators.

As a band and as artists, they took lots of creative risks. Nowhere is that more apparent than on their eighth album *Sgt. Pepper's Lonely Hearts Club Band*, which came out in 1967.

As McCartney said in an interview on the album's 50th anniversary, people tried to stop them from pushing boundaries. "We were always being told, 'You're gonna lose all your fans with this one,'" he said. "And we'd say, 'Well, we'll lose some, but we'll gain some.' We've gotta advance."

For a taste of how kaleidoscopic *Sgt. Pepper's Lonely Hearts Club Band* really is, listen to "LUCY IN THE SKY WITH DIAMONDS." The song was written by John Lennon, and listening to it is like falling into a kooky dreamland. The lyrics don't make much sense, yet you understand them. The harmonies swim around in your head like a school of fish.

On their next album, which most people call *The White Album*, they continued to flex their creative muscles. But that didn't mean adding even more bells and whistles to their creations. They still understood how powerful good music and lyrics could be. Listen to "BLACKBIRD." It's one of their most timeless songs. The only things you hear in the song are guitar and Paul McCartney's voice. It might make you cry.

THE
BEATLES

The band has a song for virtually every mood you can think of. Beatles music makes you believe you can do anything and that creativity is limitless.

ELLA FITZGERALD
BORN: April 25, 1917
HOMETOWN: Newport News,
Virginia, USA
ALBUMS SOLD: 40 million
AWARDS WON: 14 Grammy
Awards; the National Medal
of Arts

GET CREATIVE WITH

ELLA FITZGERALD

TO UNDERSTAND THE GENIUS OF ELLA FITZGERALD, YOU SHOULD LISTEN TO HER VERSION OF "HOW HIGH THE MOON" ON HER 1960 LIVE ALBUM, *ELLA IN BERLIN*.

It starts with a minute of Ella singing perfectly in pitch. Then it breaks into about six full minutes of the jazz icon's signature scatting. Scat singing is when a singer makes up melodies and words on the spot that interact with what the band is playing. It might sound a little strange, but if anyone can convince you that it's fantastic, it's Ella Fitzgerald. On this particular recording, she's undeniably incredible at it. Close your eyes as her voice swoops like an ice skater around a frozen pond in soaring patterns, sometimes fast and sometimes slow, but always effortlessly.

Ella knew that to become the best at what she did, she would have to be as creative as possible. She often mimicked the instruments in her band with her voice. "A lot of singers think all they have to do is exercise their tonsils to get ahead," she once said. "They refuse to look for new ideas and new outlets, so they fall by the wayside... I'm going to try to find out the new ideas before the others do."

The key to her genius was taking the American songbook and turning it on its head: viewing the songs through her special lens, complete with lots of scatting and putting a ton of emotion into the songs that wasn't there before. In 1958 Fitzgerald became the first Black woman to win a Grammy Award. But before concerts in Berlin and a unique legacy as an American hero, she was a girl singing for spare change on the streets of New York City. In 1934 she went onstage at the famous Apollo Theater's amateur night and tore the house down with two performances. She won the night. The interesting thing was, she didn't even intend to sing that night. She was going to dance for the audience but changed her mind when she saw there were too many dancers already performing that night. When everyone went left, Ella Fitzgerald always went right.

ELTON JOHN
BORN: March 25, 1947
HOMETOWN: Pinner, Middlesex, England
ALBUMS SOLD: 300 million
AWARDS WON: 6 Grammy Awards;
1 Academy Award

GET CREATIVE WITH

ELTON JOHN

ELTON JOHN'S CAREER REALLY TOOK OFF WHEN HE MET BERNIE TAUPIN IN 1967.

The two amateur musicians answered the same newspaper ad looking for songwriters. Elton didn't have the skills to write lyrics, and Bernie couldn't write melodies. They met up and quickly became best friends. Each had the essential talent that the other didn't. The two teamed up and have worked on more than 30 albums together over 50 years, including Elton's best, *Goodbye Yellow Brick Road.*

Listen to "BENNIE AND THE JETS" from that album. It's a demonstration of their perfect partnership. It starts with Elton hitting some awe-inspiring piano chords that make your ears perk up immediately. Then he sings Taupin's words and creates this wonderful fairy tale about a fake band called Bennie and the Jets. It's totally odd, but you just want to scream all the words along with him and dance around like a dizzy ballerina.

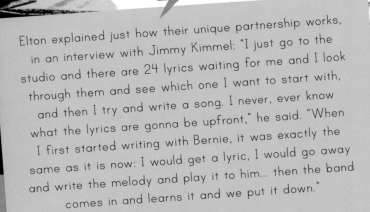

Elton explained just how their unique partnership works, in an interview with Jimmy Kimmel: "I just go to the studio and there are 24 lyrics waiting for me and I look through them and see which one I want to start with, and then I try and write a song. I never, ever know what the lyrics are gonna be upfront," he said. "When I first started writing with Bernie, it was exactly the same as it is now: I would get a lyric, I would go away and write the melody and play it to him... then the band comes in and learns it and we put it down."

THIS SECTION IS ALL ABOUT LOVE:
LOVING YOURSELF, YOUR ART, YOUR
COMMUNITY, AND—OF COURSE—
THAT CUTE PERSON YOU'VE JUST
STARTED HANGING OUT WITH.

FALL IN LOVE TO...

FALL IN LOVE TO

MARIAH CAREY

IN TERMS OF LEGENDARY SONGWRITERS, MARIAH CAREY MIGHT JUST BE IN A CLASS OF HER OWN.

She's responsible for writing almost all of her 18 songs that hit number one on the US singles chart. How does she constantly create so many songs that resonate with people? By writing songs about love and real-life experiences that everyone can attach themselves to. At first, people at her record label were unsure about letting her take so much control over her own sound, but with continued success and industry-defining decisions—she practically invented the remix!—she proved that she's a creative force to be reckoned with. Listening to Mariah Carey is like it's Christmas every day of the year.

Mariah constantly preaches to everyone that they should be confident in their songwriting, and all creative abilities.

"Don't let anyone dissuade you," she said in 2018 to Genius HQ, "or say, like, 'Let somebody else write songs for you. You are a great singer, you don't need to write your songs.' People do that to a lot of young singers, so they can be in control of what they do or make the money [by] placing songs for their friends or themselves, take their publishing. Just hold on to your publishing and make sure if you want to write that you take that opportunity to express yourself and write your songs."

To get a taste of how outstanding a Mariah Carey love song can be, listen to "WE BELONG TOGETHER." It's one of her best songs and you know just from the first few piano notes that you're going to feel it. Throughout the song Mariah pleads with her boyfriend, but the reason the song works is because it constantly hits back at how empty she feels without that special person in her life. Even if you've never been in that exact situation, Mariah's lyrics, whether they are about being restless at night because something's bothering her, or crying because she misses a person, are something anyone can tap into. It's only a bonus that her voice floats over the beat like a butterfly. You can practically hear the longing in her voice, so gorgeous and sad at the same time.

MARIAH CAREY

BORN: March 27, 1969 or 1970 (she has never confirmed)

HOMETOWN: Huntington, New York, USA

ALBUMS SOLD: 200 million

AWARDS WON: 5 Grammy Awards

FRANK OCEAN
BORN: October 28, 1987
HOMETOWN: Long Beach, California, USA
ESSENTIAL ALBUM: Blonde
AWARDS WON: 2 Grammy Awards

FALL IN LOVE TO

FRANK OCEAN

LOVING YOURSELF, RATHER THAN WORRYING WHAT OTHERS THINK, WILL ALWAYS BE THE MOST IMPORTANT THING.

It's a constant effort to look at yourself in the mirror and ask: am I being the most honest and authentic version of myself? Frank Ocean is an artist who has always tried to do that in his music and life.

After a period of success, he went into hiding a bit and reevaluated what he wanted to create. He spent a long time in London discovering work by photographers that stretched his mind. In a 2019 interview with *Gayletter* magazine he said of that period of his life, "Any time you're working in that space, around a lot of artists, they're showing you what moves them, what formed their voice over time. And it's that ritual of sharing that puts you on a whole bunch of other [stuff] you've never seen."

In an open letter on his Tumblr in 2012, he told the world that he had fallen in love with a man at one point and addressed the world about it beautifully. "Whoever you are," he wrote. "Wherever you are… I'm starting to think we're a lot alike. Human beings spinning on blackness. All wanting to be seen, touched, heard, paid attention to." He then released *Channel Orange*, his proper debut album and considered by many to be a masterpiece. It contains one of the best love songs of all time, called "THINKIN BOUT YOU." It's a stunning admission of love. Frank's voice on the song is so fragile and his falsetto (high voice) is just marvelous. Listening to Frank Ocean is like reading a letter from a friend who's been traveling all over and has so many fascinating stories to tell you.

Through other people's art and introspection, Frank Ocean has always aimed to better himself and has shown his fans that they should be doing the same. There's so much art in the world to fall in love with, and it might just reveal truths about yourself that you didn't know were there.

FALL IN LOVE TO

Troye Sivan

FOR AUSTRALIAN POP STAR TROYE SIVAN, THERE WEREN'T REALLY THAT MANY PEOPLE TO LOOK UP TO.

Troye is an internationally famous gay pop star, and there haven't been too many of them in the history of modern music.

TROYE SIVAN
BORN: June 5, 1995
HOMETOWN: Perth, Western Australia
ESSENTIAL ALBUM: Blue Neighborhood
*BONUS FACT: Troye does 10 pushups
backstage before every show.*

He told *Billboard* magazine, "I'm lucky enough to exist in 2018 where I have a record label that's like, 'Write whatever you want to write.' I don't have to hide anything. I'm honored to have this opportunity to write an album about my relationship, but in the process, be writing an album that I'm hoping is going to mean more, because I didn't have albums like that growing up. Just by the nature of who I am, the idea of writing openly and not watering stuff down for a straight audience ... If I'm being honest about my life then, you know, I am writing about nights like [ones in] 'MY MY MY!' or 'BLOOM.'"

Those songs he mentioned in his quote are two of his best love songs and he couldn't have made them without really being who he wanted to be. Listen to "My My My!" It's a song about not being afraid to be in love any more. It's like an absolute celebration. You could also try "DANCE TO THIS," a collaboration with Ariana Grande. Listening to some Troye Sivan songs is like being at a huge party where everyone is allowed to do whatever they want.

Other songs are the exact opposite and explore what it's like being extremely heartbroken. Listen to his debut album *Blue Neighborhood* for some of that. For Troye to be singing those songs about other boys is becoming less of a big deal as time goes on, but his bravery and his craftsmanship are to be admired. His songs are for everyone, though, and proof that it doesn't matter what pronouns you use in a love song, it's still a love song.

FALL IN LOVE TO

SZA

LOVE ISN'T ALWAYS JUST ABOUT A PERSON-TO-PERSON CONNECTION. IT COULD BE ABOUT TRULY LOVING WHAT YOU CREATE.

For SZA, the fight to release her debut album *Ctrl* in 2017 was very real. It took years and years to record and perfect. It was scheduled to be released several times, and then wouldn't come out. The incredibly frustrating series of events was tough, and at times she even wanted to give up entirely. "I actually quit," she tweeted at one point. But when the album came out, it was an immediate smash and it catapulted SZA into fame and critical recognition. Her love of her songs and music transcended all the obstacles and the world saw her for who she is. The love that exists in yourself for your creations is worth a little pain to get it out there.

A track like "DREW BARRYMORE," an incredibly vulnerable song where SZA confronts weaknesses in letting people control her, allows you to sympathize with her pain and your own. The song is named after the movie star for a reason: you get the same deep feeling as watching one of Barrymore's emotional films. The reason SZA fought so hard for these songs and for her career is because of what her songs do for other people.

"When I'm looking at someone in a crowd," SZA said to *Pitchfork* in 2017, "and I can see their face and I'm confident in the way that I'm talking to them when I sing, I'm like, 'I know you need me right now. I'm gonna pay attention to you. I want you to know that I see you and I'm talking to you.' I can see in their face that they're really [messed] up in that moment of whatever we're talking about in the song, or however the music makes them feel, and they just need to be with me."

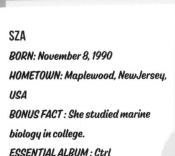

SZA
BORN: *November 8, 1990*
HOMETOWN: *Maplewood, New Jersey, USA*
BONUS FACT: *She studied marine biology in college.*
ESSENTIAL ALBUM: *Ctrl*

FALL IN LOVE TO

Carly Rae Jepsen

CARLY RAE JEPSEN
BORN: November 21, 1985
HOMETOWN: Mission, British Columbia, Canada
ESSENTIAL ALBUM: Emotion
AWARDS WON: 3 Juno Awards; 2 Billboard Music Awards

IF ALIENS EVER COME DOWN TO EARTH AND THEY NEED TO KNOW WHAT IT'S LIKE TO HAVE A WILD CRUSH, THEY'D ONLY NEED 3 MINUTES AND 13 SECONDS FOR A FULL EXPLANATION.

That's the exact run time of Carly Rae Jepsen's "CALL ME MAYBE." It's a super popular song that inspired many covers and fan-made dance videos when it came out in 2012. It's a love song that's nearly impossible not to like. The music and lyrics together paint a picture of what it's like to be someone's secret admirer and those first few stressful steps you take to get them to notice you.

The strings that play throughout the song sound like a nervously beating heart. Then, Carly takes you on a whirlwind journey about a dreamy crush, and how she waits for their phone call. It feels like it could've been written in any decade since the telephone was invented or in the future when we won't even need phones. Carly's music makes you feel like love is all around you. She's an expert songwriter and has spoken brilliantly about it in interviews.

In 2019, she told *GQ*, "I don't know that I believe in falling automatically in love. But I have *thought* that I have fallen automatically in love before. Songwriting is like indulging that feeling and hoping that you're not alone in it."

For more CRJ, you should listen to "RUN AWAY WITH ME" from her album *Emotion*. It's another song about an insanely dreamy love story. Pay attention to the horns that open the song: they're wild, and they sound like your brain is about to explode with heart emojis. Also try out "I REALLY LIKE YOU," a pretty straightforward song about, well...when you really, really like someone. You can probably sing along with her the very first time you hear it, and that just feels good.

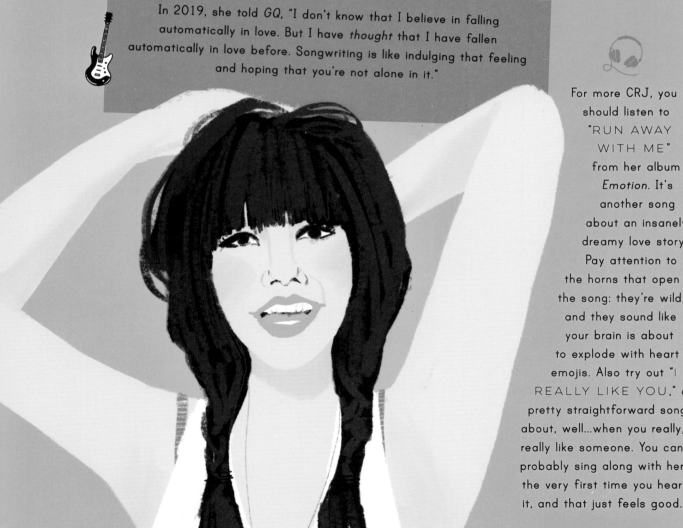

FALL IN LOVE TO

BILLY JOEL

SOME OF BILLY JOEL'S SONGS ARE PERFECT LOVE SONGS—ROMANTIC, WARM MESSAGES TO LOVERS AND FRIENDS.

For one of those, listen to "JUST THE WAY YOU ARE." It's been played at an unknowable number of weddings because it's super easy to listen to and makes you feel warm and fuzzy inside. Listen to the way he plays the piano. Even if it's your first time consciously listening to it, it seems like you've known the song your entire life.

BILLY JOEL
BORN: May 9, 1949
HOMETOWN: Hicksville, New York, USA
ALBUMS SOLD: 150 million
AWARDS WON: 5 Grammys; Rock and Roll Hall of Fame

He hasn't released a new album of original material since 1993's *River of Dreams*, but the singer-songwriter is currently more popular than at pretty much any point of his career. He has a monthly residency at New York City's Madison Square Garden, where he runs through his impressive catalog of hits for his fans. He's currently 70 years old and has played the venue over 100 times now, an insane run that's unmatched by his peers. They even raised his "jersey" into the rafters of the building as if he is a star athlete. But even though he isn't actively recording music, he still sits down at the piano pretty much every day and works on new music.

"I write," he said in a 2018 interview with the *NYT*. "I continue to write the music. I develop it, I do expositions, variations. But I haven't recorded it. I haven't even notated it. It's all here [taps his head]."

That love of songwriting and playing the piano has been the driving force of his music for almost 50 years of his career. To understand Billy Joel, you should listen to his most famous song, "PIANO MAN." It's a love song about a bar and all of the patrons who go there. His songwriting is so cinematic, you can picture every little nook and cranny of the place.

But all Billy Joel songs are love songs, really, because for a piano-playing superstar like him, it's all about the love of his craft.

FALL IN LOVE TO ELVIS

ELVIS
BORN: January 8, 1935
HOMETOWN: Tupelo, Mississippi, USA
ALBUMS SOLD: 1 billion
AWARDS WON: The US Presidential Medal of Freedom

"CAN'T HELP FALLING IN LOVE" MIGHT BE THE MOST FAMOUS LOVE SONG OF ALL TIME.

It was originally recorded by Elvis Presley in 1961 for a movie he starred in called *Blue Hawaii*. For Elvis, a man generally credited for popularizing rock and roll music around the world, the song was almost always the last song he played in concerts. People really freaked out. Listening to the song, and Elvis's music in general, there's just an indescribable power to it that compels you to want to hear more and more.

Look online for footage of Elvis singing it in 1968, as part of a TV special often referred to as his "Comeback Special." Some background: Elvis was one of the most famous stars in the world. He had revolutionized music with his hip-moving dancing and then eventually broke into acting, which took over his career. Unfortunately, he had done some bad roles and was a bit down on his luck. But watching his performance of "Can't Help Falling in Love" at the special, you'd never really know it. He belts his way through the song while staring intensely at the close-up audience, and you can cut the tension in the room with a knife. It's kind of startling to watch. With the special, the world once again took Elvis in as the star he was.

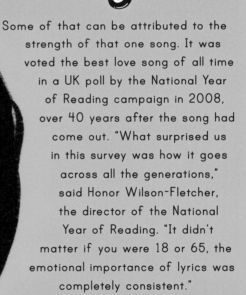

Some of that can be attributed to the strength of that one song. It was voted the best love song of all time in a UK poll by the National Year of Reading campaign in 2008, over 40 years after the song had come out. "What surprised us in this survey was how it goes across all the generations," said Honor Wilson-Fletcher, the director of the National Year of Reading. "It didn't matter if you were 18 or 65, the emotional importance of lyrics was completely consistent."

That speaks to how powerful a silly love song can be. Often we think of love as something to be dismissed but if the lyrics—poetry, really—can stick with a population for multiple generations, then we should never ignore the power and potential of love.

John Legend

FOR SONGS ABOUT LOVING THE WORLD, YOU DON'T NEED TO LOOK ANY FURTHER THAN JOHN LEGEND.

JOHN LEGEND
BORN: December 28, 1978
HOMETOWN: Springfield, Ohio, USA
ESSENTIAL ALBUM: Get Lifted
AWARDS WON: 10 Grammy Awards, 1 Oscar, 1 Tony, 1 Emmy; EGOT! (acronym for "Emmy, Grammy, Oscar, Tony")

His voice sounds sweet as honey and his lyrics are so brutally honest that they might make you cry. Listening to John Legend is like being wrapped up in a billion blankets. Listen to "ALL OF ME." It's a song he wrote about his wife Chrissy Teigen, and it's filled with the kind of things we should all be so lucky to have our partners say about us. Legend is an incredibly talented piano player as well, and this song features some of his smoothest playing.

But what makes Legend so special is that he couples those one-on-one love songs with a different kind of love song—that shows love to his community.

"Every artist has to make a choice about what their story is, what they want to say," he told WSJ. magazine. "Part of what makes a great artist is honesty on all sorts of levels—being honest about what's going on in your mind and how you interact with other people, in love and friendships and family and all sorts of things. The best artists create beautiful work based on their truth, and my truth includes talking about what's happening in the world right now."

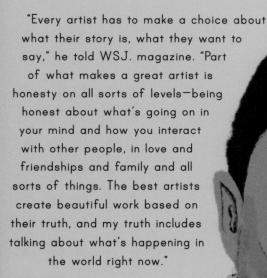

When you listen to a song of his like "PREACH," those same emotions from his love songs—tenderness, truthfulness, and empathy—are still there, but he uses them differently. Instead of making one person feel good, he's trying to uplift a ton of others alongside him. It's a modern protest song, using love and hope as very powerful weapons. The same could be said about one of his first hits, "ORDINARY PEOPLE." It's maybe his most elegant song, piano-wise. The melody is so calming. In the lyrics of the verse, he's talking to his partner, but in the chorus, his message is that we're all human beings, just trying to figure everything out. Yes, it's a song for one person, but it's meant to help so many others too.

WHEN THERE'S NO ONE ELSE
YOU CAN POSSIBLY BE
OTHER THAN YOU,

BE YOURSELF WITH...

BE YOURSELF WITH

DAVID BOWIE

TO UNDERSTAND HOW UNIQUE DAVID BOWIE IS AND WAS, YOU ONLY HAVE TO LOOK AT ONE PICTURE OF HIM.

Specifically, the cover of his 1973 album *Aladdin Sane*. The title is the name of one of the more famous characters that he invented. In that image, Bowie is Aladdin, skin all silver, and hair a blaze of fire. Then there's the lightning bolt painted across his face that catches your eye and makes you turn your head. Who is this guy?

David Bowie also explored characters such as lost astronauts—a glamorous rock star named Ziggy Stardust—and many more. There is a slightly off quality to all David Bowie's music—like he's winking at you and letting you know that you're on the inside of the joke. Along the way he blended rock and roll with soul, pop, and just about anything else you can think of—with great results.

"Music has given me over 40 years of extraordinary experiences," he said. "I can't say that life's pains or more tragic episodes have been diminished because of it. But it's allowed me so many moments of companionship when I've been lonely and a sublime means of communication when I wanted to touch people. It's been both my doorway of perception and the house that I live in."

Listen to "SPACE ODDITY." It's a song about being completely stranded in space. It's the craziest science fiction opera ever. In contrast, there's "CHANGES." It feels like it was made for everyone on Earth to feel inspired. "YOUNG AMERICANS" captur[es] everything special abou[t] David Bowie: the lyrics a[re] so far out and Bowie's snarling delivery really carries the whole thing home. Backed by a soulful chorus of singers, he sounds like the leader of the coolest church in the universe.

DAVID BOWIE
BORN: January 8, 1974
HOMETOWN: London, England
ALBUMS SOLD: 140 million
AWARDS WON: Rock and Roll Hall of Fame; 6 Grammy Awards

BE YOURSELF WITH

CHRISTINE AND THE QUEENS

THE WAY EVERYONE PRESENTS THEMSELVES TO THE WORLD IS A CONSTANTLY
CHANGING THING.

Sometimes it's in our appearance: the way we wear our clothes or the way we cut
our hair. Other times it can be the things we're born with or the feelings that are
inside of us. Luckily, if we don't like the way we're presenting something about
ourselves, we can change it. French singer Héloïse Letissier, otherwise known as
Chris, is someone who knows that better than anyone. Throughout her life and
her career, she's matched up her persona, her music, and her sound with how
she's feeling inside. Sometimes she feels like a boy, sometimes like a girl, and
sometimes in the middle or neither at all—she's someone truly original.

CHRISTINE AND THE QUEENS

BORN: June 1, 1988
HOMETOWN: Nantes, France
ESSENTIAL ALBUM: Chaleur Humaine
BONUS FACT: When she writes music, she visualizes the choreography that's going to go with every song.

"I was never sure of how to be a man or a woman," she said in an early
interview. "Because I felt that being a woman was an obstacle, I wanted
to become gender-neutral. It became my way of tricking the system."

You can hear it in her song "TILTED." It's
a perfectly titled song. The beat sounds like
floating back and forth, and maybe upside-down
on an extremely chill boat. Her voice is soft and
rises high above the beat and she later drifts
into rapping fast as hell in French. There are
so many different versions of herself on the
song. Then listen to "GOYA SODA" from her
second album, simply called, *Chris*. She's a lot
harder and more intense than on "Tilted," but still
has moments where her voice sounds angelic.
Listening to Christine and the Queens can be kind
of an eye-opening experience—a transformation
that's really fun to dance along to. Like her, you
might find yourself going against what people
think you should be like. It's always necessary for
you to feel comfortable in your own skin.

BE YOURSELF WITH

KELIS

KELIS
BORN: *August 21, 1979*
HOMETOWN: *New York, New York, USA*
ALBUMS SOLD: *6 million +*
ESSENTIAL ALBUM: *Tasty*

KELIS IS PROBABLY MOST FAMOUS FOR HER ICONIC SONG "MILKSHAKE."

The chorus has been stuck in practically the entire world's head since it came out in 2003. Yes, its lyrics are fun to sing along to, but it's the beat that makes the song irresistible: a fiesta of a million drums and chimes all at once. It's a classic at any party.

But Kelis is so much more than just that one hit. On pretty much all of her albums, she's reinvented herself and shown everyone a different side of her artistry. On *Tasty*, that's the one with "Milkshake" on it, she made an innovative version of 2000s R&B. "SUGAR HONEY ICED TEA" is another perfect song she made at that time. But on *Flesh Tone*, she's a dance-floor diva: listen to "4TH OF JULY (FIREWORKS)" for a taste of that style. On *Food*, she's a jazzy impresario, making songs that sound super classic but still new. Listen to all of the horns on the album—they're exceptionally arresting, especially on "BREAKFAST."

Another great thing about Kelis is that, although she's a musical chameleon, she didn't stop herself from accomplishing other goals in her life, like going to culinary school and becoming a real chef.

"My mother is a chef and my father is a musician, so music and food have always been a part of my life," she said.

After training, she released her own sauce line and started living and working on a farm to be more connected to her food. In life, and in music, Kelis stands alone as someone who always does as she pleases and makes sure to acknowledge and nurture all of her different thoughts and visions.

BE YOURSELF WITH

Björk

BJÖRK
BORN: November 21, 1965
HOMETOWN: Reykjavík, Iceland
ALBUMS SOLD: 30+ million
AWARDS WON: 5 BRIT Awards

POP MUSIC IS REALLY FUN, BUT SOMETIMES YOU WANT SOMETHING NOT ON THE EASY LEVEL.

For when you want to challenge yourself, there's Björk. She's an artist from Iceland, but the music she makes might as well be from Mars—if Mars had an insanely good dance club that was also a museum of art that blows your mind. Listen to "HUMAN BEHAVIOR," one of her earliest songs. At certain points it sounds like she's singing notes you've never really heard before—but none of them sound wrong, just different.

Because she grew up as an outsider, Björk was able to craft her own image and stand alone.

"When I was growing up, I always had this feeling that I had been dropped in from somewhere else," she said to *i-D magazine* in 1993. "That was how I was treated at school in Iceland where the kids used to call me 'China girl' and everybody thought I was unusual because I was Chinese. It gave me room to do my own thing. If I can get the space I need to do my own thing by being called an alien, an elf, a China girl or whatever, then that's great! I think I've only realized in the past few years what a comfortable situation that is." Finding "comfort" in being considered "not normal" takes a lot of work, but Björk's obviously found so much reward there.

To try and meet Björk at her level, you probably should listen to an album of her work all at once. It's almost like a movie. Try her 1995 album *Post*. It's got a lot of styles to it, so you may be able to latch on to something and branch out from there. There's club music, showtunesy music, and moving ballads: a little something for everyone.

BE YOURSELF WITH

Dolly Parton

DOLLY PARTON
BORN: January 19, 1946
HOMETOWN: Pittman Center,
Tennessee, USA
ALBUMS SOLD: 160+ million
AWARDS WON: 8 Grammy Awards;
Country Music Hall of Fame

EVERY SINGLE THING DOLLY PARTON HAS EVER SAID IS RIDICULOUSLY QUOTABLE.

A small selection: "The way I see it, if you want the rainbow, you gotta put up with the rain," "Storms make trees take deeper roots," and of course, "It costs a lot of money to look this cheap." But one of her most famous quotes that really illustrates who she is as an artist and person is: "Find out who you are and do it on purpose." It's a brilliant life philosophy; live as your most authentic self, with the volume turned all the way up.

And so when you see Dolly Parton, there's no mistaking her for anyone else. Her blond hair is piled sky-high, her makeup is always on full blast, and her smile is wide as the horizon. She's usually wearing at least one thing with a bit of sparkle too. It's a glorious look, and under all that sheen is real, mind-blowing talent.

Parton is one of the most accomplished songwriters of all time. She's written well over 3,000 songs. Her version—the original!—of "I WILL ALWAYS LOVE YOU" will probably make you weep. Listen to the frailty in her voice and it's sure to move you. "9 TO 5" is a completely different mode from her: it's goofy and angry all at the same time, which seems impossible, but if anyone can do that, it's Dolly. "JOLENE" is probably one of the best songs ever written. The guitar that leads the song is addictive to listen to and Dolly's voice is enchanting. By the end of the final chorus you'll be begging Jolene to leave Dolly's man alone too.

Listening to Dolly Parton is like sitting down with an old friend who has an endless list of stories to catch you up on.

BE YOURSELF WITH

OUTKAST

ANDRÉ "ANDRÉ 3000" BENJAMIN AND ANTWAN "BIG BOI" PATTON MET WHEN THEY WERE 16 AT THEIR LOCAL MALL IN ATLANTA.

The two talented teenage rappers quickly bonded over their love of music and formed a duo together called OutKast. In 1994 they released their debut album *Southernplayalisticadillacmuzik*. It sounded like nothing that had come before it. Truthfully, it sounded like Atlanta, a one-of-a-kind thing that drew in all types of Southern traditions to make something that no one else could imitate. They immediately became the first real rap superstars of the South.

At a big hip-hop awards show a year later, OutKast won the award for Best New Rap Group. The crowd—largely made up of rappers and fans from the Northeast Coast and the West Coast—started booing them as André and Big Boi took the stage.

Years later, Big Boi recounted to *Vibe* magazine what happened next. "Dre got upset, and he said, 'I'm gon' tell y'all something, the South got something to say.' From that point forward, all that hate was just motivation for us... We were working at Stankonia studios, the studio we have now. And we just started recording record after record."

They never let what people thought of their hometown get in the way of their success. They showed the world just how special Atlanta is through their music. When you listen to OutKast, you can see that there's a bigger world outside where you're from. Listen to "MS. JACKSON," from their 2000 album *Stankonia* to get a sense of what their music is like. The hook is catchy, the beat makes you feel like you're in a dream, and André and Big Boi play off each other. There's also "HEY YA" and "THE WAY YOU MOVE," from their double album of solo projects, *Speakerboxxx/ The Love Below*. There's not another song in the world that sounds like either of them, and that's what makes them so special.

OUTKAST

HOMETOWN: Atlanta, Georgia, USA

BONUS FACT: According to astrologers, Big Boi's star sign is Aquarius and André's is Gemini, perfectly balancing each other out.

ALBUMS SOLD: 25 million +

AWARDS WON: 6 Grammy Awards

Ryuichi Sakamoto

THERE'S SOMETHING ABOUT THE WAY
RYUICHI SAKAMOTO PLAYS PIANO THAT'S
JUST SPELLBINDING.

A lot of his compositions are used as scores
for films and there's a reason why—they sound
cinematic. Listen to "MERRY CHRISTMAS MR.
LAWRENCE," a piece he wrote for a movie of
the same name. It starts off surprisingly strong, but
not in a bad way, like a quick breeze in the summer
heat. Then slowly, the song turns triumphant and
ensnares you. Sakamoto's playing is so meaningful,
you can almost picture characters and scenes in your
mind without seeing the movie at all.

There's
a relaxing quality
to his playing, too. A lot
of that can be attributed to
the way he sometimes doesn't
play any notes at all. Listen for
the silence in his pieces: he
uses pauses and changes
of tempo like nobody
else can.

"Why do I want
to play much slower than
before?," he once said. "Because
I wanted to hear the resonance.
I want to have less notes and more
spaces. Spaces, not silence. Space is
resonant, is still ringing. I want to enjoy
that resonance, to hear it growing,
then the next sound, and the next
note or harmony can come.
That's exactly what I
want."

For more of
Sakamoto's work listen to
"M.A.Y. IN THE BACKYARD,"
a track he first released in 1996, on an
album called *1996*. It starts off fast and
choppy, which makes your ears perk up. Then
dizzying strings come in. What comes next is
wild—it's like you're being whisked away in a
tornado and into a world of chaos, until you're
back at a restful place. Then the process
repeats itself and you're on the journey
all over again. Being able to transport
someone on that journey is a real
talent, and Sakamoto has
it in spades.

RYUICHI SAKAMOTO
BORN: *January 17, 1952*
HOMETOWN: *Tokyo, Japan*
ESSENTIAL ALBUM: *1996*
AWARDS WON: *1 Grammy Award*

CHILL OUT TO

SUFJAN STEVENS

LISTENING TO SUFJAN STEVENS IS LIKE HAVING A REALLY DEEP CONVERSATION WITH A FRIEND YOU CAN TRUST.

His music is sometimes folky, at other times rocky, and has even been electronic, too. But one thing is continual in his music: emotional honesty. No matter what it sounds like, the relief his music provides is like a good deep breath. Listen to "SHOULD HAVE KNOWN BETTER." The guitar is twinkly and his voice whispers calmly. It's a song about his mom and finding some personal peace after she passed away. If you're going through a difficult time, it can make you feel better. If you're not in the mood for soft guitars, listen to "IMPOSSIBLE SOUL," from his 2010 album *Age of Adz*. It's almost 26 minutes long, and it's like an explosion of sounds including cymbals, orchestras, and loud choruses. But still, his voice floats above the chaos and gives you a message to sink your teeth into.

Not surprisingly, Sufjan is always aware of the importance of his words and his music and what they provide for his fans.

"Artists can be categorized as political leaders, and sages, and prophets, but the work outlives the vessel of the work," he said to *Pitchfork* in 2017. "The poetry outlives the poet. I really believe in that. But while I'm alive, I'll keep at it. I feel incredible gratitude to have the opportunity to create and to be part of that process. Especially now that I'm older, I don't really feel like I have to prove myself any more. I just have to be a steward and try to make the best work possible. If I can also be an example, great, but really it's about the creative endeavor for me. It never feels easy, but it always feels necessary to be creating work and making music."

SUFJAN STEVENS
BORN: July 1, 1975
HOMETOWN: Detroit, Michigan, USA
ESSENTIAL ALBUM: Carrie & Lowell
BONUS FACT: He was once rumored to be working on 50 different albums for all of the US states.

Stevie Wonder

SOME SONGS ARE SO LOVELY THAT LISTENING TO THEM IS LIKE BEING WRAPPED UP IN A FUZZY BLANKET.

Pretty much every song on Stevie Wonder's *Songs in the Key of Life* is like that. There's a reason so many of his songs get played at weddings and special family events: they're audio comfort food. Listen to the opening of that album, "LOVE'S IN NEED OF LOVE TODAY." From the floating harmonies that open the track to the slow organ that guides it, it's like someone is wrapping you in a tight hug, telling you it's all going to be okay.

The range of emotion on display on this album is astounding. "SIR DUKE," a tribute to jazz legend Duke Ellington, is a powerful meditation on how valued music itself can be. The bass line in "I WISH" is one of the most joyous grooves ever and so fun to dance to. "KNOCKS ME OFF MY FEET" is a stunning love song. This is all just one of his albums, too. With Stevie Wonder, there's an endless trove of treasures to dig through and discover.

Stevie Wonder is a master of so many things; playing piano, blowing the harmonica, but especially songwriting. He's able to convey so many earnest feelings through his songs. His songwriting skills are unmatched. Even the way he talks about crafting his music and how songs come to him is exquisite.

"To this day, I never sit down and formally write songs," he said to the *Wall Street Journal*. "They emerge from the process of listening to what I'm doing on the keyboard. I just play and songs sort of happen. Like a painter, I get my inspiration from experiences that can be painful or beautiful. I always start from a feeling of profound gratitude... And write from there."

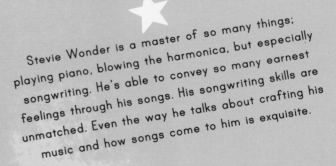

STEVIE WONDER
BORN: May 13, 1950
HOMETOWN: Saginaw, Michigan, USA
ALBUMS SOLD: 100 million
AWARDS WON: 25 Grammy Awards, 1 Academy Award

CHILL OUT TO

FLEETWOOD MAC

FLEETWOOD MAC
HOMETOWN:
London, England
ALBUMS SOLD:
100 million
ESSENTIAL ALBUM:
Rumors
AWARDS WON:
1 Grammy Award

IT CAN BE HARD TO GET ALONG WITH FRIENDS AND LOVED ONES SOMETIMES.

No one knows that better than the members of Fleetwood Mac. After a lot of lineup changes in the early 70s, the band really got off the ground in 1975 when guitarist Lindsey Buckingham and singer Stevie Nicks joined the group, and they released a self-titled album. The 1977 follow-up, called *Rumors*, is an incredible album that details all of the drama that went on inside the band. The lyrics are all about the fighting, breakups, and make-ups between the band members, but the music is pure bliss. Definitely listen to the whole thing, but you'd be hard-pressed to find a song more gorgeous than "DREAMS." Stevie Nicks's voice is super smoky and mysterious—the lyrics are too!—but the drums are clear as a bell. Listening to Fleetwood Mac is a very cool experience that is a one-of-a-kind sort of thing.

Through the years, the band has broken up several times, but their chemistry together has always been completely undeniable. The band's history is a reminder that hot feelings and tensions can make something divine, and that over time, you can grow to understand others better.

Surprisingly, with all of the drama going on, Stevie Nicks says the album was super fun to record. "We were all writing little movies around what was really happening, and we were digging it," she said. "We were having a lot of fun recording those songs, even though we were falling apart ... if anything was keeping us from falling apart, it was going into the studio every day. And we were totally having a great time."

BEFORE AN EXAM, RECITAL,
PARTY, OR ANYTHING
WHERE YOU NEED ENERGY,

GET PUMPED UP WITH...

GET PUMPED UP WITH

DRAKE

FOR DRAKE, CONFIDENCE COMES FROM WITHIN.

The Canadian rapper started his career as an actor and slowly transitioned into making music. His first couple of songs caught the ear of superstar rapper Lil Wayne, who mentored him and gave him a record deal. Through continued work with his best friend and producer Noah "40" Shebib, he became one of the most successful rappers of his generation. In almost all of his songs, Drake is always reminding himself that he came from smaller circumstances and to keep his loved ones as close as possible. Listening to Drake can make you feel like a superhero whose enemies have all teamed up to defeat you. If you believe in yourself, though, you can rise above all that.

Drake was part of a wave of rappers who also sang their own hooks, and no one excelled at it like Drake. Listen to "IN MY FEELINGS" from his 2018 album *Scorpion*. It's a perfect example of why he's so great. His voice is sugary sweet as his sings to a woman named Kiki and then super chill when he's rapping. The beat is inspired by a style of music called New Orleans bounce. Drake is always on the hunt for a new sound, a new flow, or a new look. Take "HOTLINE BLING," for example. The beat practically sounds like something you'd hear in a waiting room. But then the drums kick in and everything changes. His voice glides all over the track and you're just in love with it out of nowhere.

"A new flow is absolutely the most crucial discovery in rap, to me," Drake once explained to *The Fader* in 2015. "Honestly, like, I love that I'm sitting here talking to you, but at the same time I don't, because I want to go to the studio, and I'm praying that 40 has a beat, so that I can do something new that I've never done before. That is my main joy in life."

DRAKE

BORN: October, 24 1986

HOMETOWN: Toronto, Ontario, Canada

ALBUMS SOLD: 150 million +

AWARDS WON: 4 Grammy Awards; 6 American Music Awards

BEYONCÉ

NO ONE WORKS AS HARD, OR SEEMS TO FIND AS MUCH JOY IN WORKING HARD, AS BEYONCÉ.

"I don't like too much structure. I like to be free," Beyoncé said to Vogue in 2018. "I'm not alive unless I am creating something. I'm not happy if I'm not creating, if I'm not dreaming, if I'm not creating a dream and making it into something real. I'm not happy if I'm not improving, evolving, moving forward, inspiring, teaching, and learning."

The Texas singer made a career for herself as part of the girl group Destiny's Child. Armed with their unbelievable voices, militant training, and a strong creative vision, they became the most successful girl group of all time. Next, it was time to go solo. Although there was still some doubt about the longevity of Beyoncé's solo career, she extinguished those opinions forever with 2003's "Crazy In Love." From the very first notes of the song—horns that sound like they're from the most holy kingdom—Beyoncé announces her arrival. The song is one of the best songs to get you moving. Without even seeing her signature choreography for the song, you just know that you need to shake every inch of your body when it comes on.

Throughout her career, Beyoncé has constantly changed the entire game. With no warning or rumors, she dropped a self-titled album in 2013 that had matching music videos for every song. She followed that up with Lemonade, in 2016, an album set to a film about her life that blew critics away. Later, she became the first Black woman to headline the American music festival Coachella, and she released a documentary all about the long process that went into her groundbreaking performance.

To listen to Beyoncé is to know that there's a better version of yourself out there somewhere just waiting to come out. All it takes is some motivation and the desire to become that better person.

BEYONCÉ
BORN: September 4, 1981
HOMETOWN: Houston, Texas, USA
ALBUMS SOLD: 100 million +
AWARDS WON: 23 Grammy Awards

GET PUMPED UP WITH

ROSALÍA

THE FIRST TIME YOU SEE SPANISH SINGER ROSALÍA IN THE VIDEO FOR "MALAMENTE," SHE'S STANDING IN A PARKING LOT WITH SIX GIRLS BEHIND HER IN A *V* FORMATION.

She's got a red track suit on and lots of gold jewelry too. It's simple, but she just looks really, really cool. Later, she's with those dancers in an open back of a truck speeding down the street—but she somehow never misses a beat. The video tells a love story and has elements of bullfighting in it too. It feels very old school and new school at the same time.

ROSALIA
BORN: September 25, 1993
HOMETOWN: Sant Esteve Sesrovires, Spain
ESSENTIAL ALBUM: El Mal Querer
BONUS FACT: Rosalía's breakthrough album was originally her senior thesis at school.

The song is in Spanish—all of her songs are—and the beat behind her on this song is a mix of American hip-hop, Latinx pop, and Flamenco, a guitar-fueled, improvisational genre that's from Spain. It looks and sounds like nothing that's come before it, and that's why it's easy to get excited about what the future holds for Rosalía.

Rosalía is aware of what she brings to the table and understands her place in the universe. "There are artists of all kinds," she said to *The Fader* in 2019. "There are artists who are here to remind us where we come from; there are artists who are here to show us where to go, you know?"

Her album *El Mal Querer* was inspired by a 13th-century novel called *Flamenca*. Throughout the album, there are moments that sound like opera, some that sound like rap, and even a Justin Timberlake sample. *El Mal Querer* is a perfect album to pore over and analyze, discovering little Easter eggs along the way. If you don't speak Spanish, go online and look up translations of her lyrics, then think about them while you listen to the emotion in her voice.

GET PUMPED UP WITH

THE ROLLING STONES

THE ROLLING STONES
HOMETOWN: *London, England*
ALBUMS SOLD: *250 million*
AWARDS WON : *3 Grammy awards*
ESSENTIAL ALBUM: *Let It Bleed*

THE ROLLING STONES BURST ONTO THE MUSIC SCENE IN THE 60S WITH PURE ROCK AND ROLL, AND AN ENERGY IN THEIR LIVE SHOWS THAT WAS UNMATCHED.

Listen to "SATISFACTION." In their huge catalog of hits, the song still stands out. From that opening guitar riff, you know it's going to be all attitude. It's a statement about getting what you want, an emotion that a lot of their songs explore. Frontman Mick Jagger sings his frustrations out while Keith Richards keeps the vibes steady on guitar. They're a classic pair and wouldn't be the icons they are today without each other.

From "BROWN SUGAR," to "PAINT IT BLACK," to "SYMPATHY FOR THE DEVIL," the band has so many hits. But their live performance style is what they're best known for. Mick Jagger is one of the most charismatic lead singers in music history. He's famous for puffing his lips, jutting his hips out, and powering around stage like he owns the building. Alongside Keith, his unique style—as well as his wild fashion sense—has inspired countless artists for decades now.

The band is still one of the biggest touring acts in the world, and Mick says they won't be stopping any time soon.

RIHANNA

RIHANNA WAS BORN IN BARBADOS AND HAD BIG DREAMS FROM THE START.

Her mom owned a beauty salon and she would hang around the store dreaming about becoming a music star. It wasn't until she won a local talent contest that she began to seriously look for success. She cut some demo songs with her friends and set out on a quest to become an established artist. Soon, she met Jay-Z in New York and he signed her to his record label.

Listen to "WE FOUND LOVE." The beat is infectious and Rihanna's voice dances over it with absolute fire behind it. Try "DIAMONDS" too. Although it's not a party song, you still feel Rih's power coming through the track. Every Rihanna song shows off a different side of the superstar that is impossible not to love. She's the coolest chameleon in music.

She also keeps her fans, who are nicknamed the Navy, waiting anxiously for more music. While achieving her childhood goals, she realized she wanted to do lots more than just release albums. And so, Rihanna created beauty and fashion lines that have become very successful. She's created an empire that just keeps growing, while maintaining her unstoppable drive.

She was a star from her first song, but by assuming creative control of her image and after rising above personal traumas in the public eye, Rihanna became an icon.

"Every time it was about challenging myself: I have to do better, I have to do better," she said. "And what's next, what's next? I won a Grammy and that was seconds into my past as soon as it got into my hands. I have to think about the next thing, which is terrible because people should live in the moment. I just started branching out into different creative outlets. That's what makes me happy."

RIHANNA
BORN: February 20, 1988
HOMETOWN: Saint Michael, Barbados
ALBUMS SOLD: 250 million
AWARDS WON: 9 Grammy Awards; 13 American Music Awards

CELEBRATE LIFE WITH

LADY GAGA

LADY GAGA HAS WORN A THOUSAND DISGUISES. SHE MADE A NAME FOR HERSELF IN THE 2000S WITH HER TREMENDOUS DANCE SONGS AND HER KOOKY FASHION.

She once wore a dress made out of meat, showed up to a red carpet inside of a dinosaur egg, and even met the Queen of England wearing red latex and sparkly eye makeup. At other points she's shifted her look and career and gone the opposite way for a while, wearing simple things like denim shorts and leather jackets.

LADY GAGA
BORN: March 28, 1986
HOMETOWN: New York, New York, USA
ALBUMS SOLD: 27 million
AWARDS WON: 9 Grammy Awards; 1 Academy Award

Even through all of her artistic phases, her music has always spoken for itself and stood up for others. Listen to "BORN THIS WAY," one of the best pop songs ever written in support of the LGBTQ+ community.

Behind the dance music and outfits, there's always been a lot of heart in her songs. "SHALLOW" from A Star Is Born, a movie that she starred in, is an example of that. You can hear all the pain in her voice.

The power in her voice comes from overcoming, and still dealing with, mental health issues. She also has a condition called fibromyalgia, which causes her a lot of pain. One time, she even had to cancel a bunch of tour dates because she needed her body to heal. But no matter what, Gaga doesn't give up: soon she was back on the road singing to her millions of fans.

She is always outspoken on mental health issues and encourages everyone around her to be strong individuals. "Depression doesn't take away your talents — it just makes them harder to find," she said to Harper's Bazaar. "But I always find it. I learned that my sadness never destroyed what was great about me. You just have to go back to that greatness, find that one little light that's left."

ARIANA GRANDE
BORN: *June 26, 1993*
HOMETOWN: *Boca Raton, Florida, USA*
ESSENTIAL ALBUM: *Sweetener*
AWARDS WON: *1 Grammy Award; 1 BRIT Award*

CELEBRATE LIFE WITH

ARIANA GRANDE

ARIANA GRANDE'S VOICE IS CLEARLY OUT OF THIS WORLD.

There are just not many people like her who can hit high notes like that. She started her career as a Broadway singer and that level of showmanship just doesn't disappear: through training and discipline, she's been able to get even better with time. On her 2019 album, titled *Thank U, Next*, she took all of that artistic growth and was able to tell stories about her life in a candid way. It took her career to a completely new place and more people began to understand the person she really is.

Listen to "BE ALRIGHT." From the opening seconds of the song you hear the celestial tones of her voice straight away. Next to the clinking piano notes they soar. The song is really fun to dance or chill to. The lyrics put your mind at ease while you get to soak up Ariana's excellence. It's effortless.

Now listen to "NO TEARS LEFT TO CRY." It's the first single she released after a difficult time in her life. It's a sonic version of seeing a rainbow after a rainstorm. It's a feel-good vibe that doesn't forget about the sadness in life. Ariana takes in her despair, looks at the world, and smiles back. It might make you smile too.

CELEBRATE LIFE WITH

Whitney Houston

WHITNEY HOUSTON
BORN: August 9, 1963
HOMETOWN: Newark,
New Jersey, USA
ALBUMS SOLD: 200 million
AWARDS WON: 7 Grammy
Awards; 1 Academy Award

TO UNDERSTAND THE POWER OF WHITNEY HOUSTON'S VOICE IS TO UNDERSTAND MUSIC ITSELF ON SOME LEVEL.

Watch her performance from the 1994 Grammy Awards. She was there to perform "I WILL ALWAYS LOVE YOU," from the film *The Bodyguard*, which she starred in. The performance starts with just her voice in a dark arena but the audience erupts into applause because they know that voice. Then Whitney appears, standing alone in a white dress, singing impeccably. About three and a half minutes in, there's the note. If you've ever heard this song, you know it, and if you don't, you certainly will. It's absolutely jaw dropping and the vocal gymnastics just carry on.

For a lighter side of Whitney, enjoy "I WANNA DANCE WITH SOMEBODY" or "HOW WILL I KNOW." Her voice still has the intensity of "I Will Always Love You" but it's used in an altogether different way. It's like running a marathon backwards.

In some ways, she is a peerless wonder. Growing up as the daughter of an accomplished singer gave her a hard childhood. Whitney was told by her mother that being a singer would be a lonely life. Whitney found that to be true, but could not deny the world her gifts. Throughout her lifetime, she dealt with inner demons of all sorts but maintained a strong sense of self, as she sings about on "GREATEST LOVE OF ALL."

Despite her troubles, she always had that voice and those songs. Nothing and no one could take that away from her.

The kind of music they make is a special brand of K-pop—that's Korean pop music—that blends the sounds of their home with the hip-hop sounds of America, and other sounds from all over the world. Listen to their song "LOVE MAZE", from their *Love Yourself* trilogy of EPs, and think about how nicely the singing and rapping blend together. In one part Jimin and Jin sing together, then pass the song to RM, who comes in with a savage rap verse.

BTS

HOMETOWN : Seoul, South Korea
ALBUMS SOLD : 15 million
BONUS FACT: Fans of BTS call themselves "ARMY."
ESSENTIAL ALBUM: BTS World

BTS all get along so well and they make sure their fans feel welcome too. In 2018, they appeared in front of government leaders from all over the world and spoke about what they want fans to get from their music: self-love. "No matter who you are," RM said, "or where you're from, your skin color, your gender identity, just speak yourself. Find your name and find your voice by speaking yourself." All of BTS stood behind him, supporting him as he spread their message of acceptance to the world.

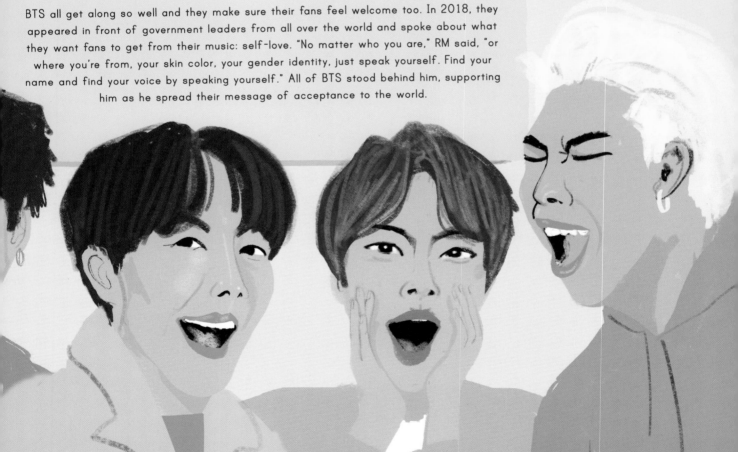

WHEN YOU'RE FEELING
POWERLESS, AGITATED,
UPSET, OR HURT,

TAKE A STAND WITH...

TAKE A STAND WITH
JOHNNY CASH

JOHNNY CASH WAS A COUNTRY LEGEND LIKE NO OTHER.

While everyone else was wearing sparkly jumpsuits with fringes, he wore all black from head to toe, earning him the nickname "The Man in Black." His songs are folksy and super honest, and they also incorporate political messages. Johnny Cash always told the world what he meant and what he stood for, especially when it came to prisons and prisoners. After seeing a movie that showed what the conditions were like in American jails in the 50s, he decided to do something about it.

Listen to his song "FOLSOM PRISON BLUES." The story he tells in the song is about an outlaw. His voice is strong and powerful as he sings about being stuck in jail. It became a favorite of a renegade crowd. Listening to Johnny Cash and his bravado can make you feel like an outlaw yourself. The most famous version of the song was recorded live at the actual Folsom Prison in front of the inmates.

That was the first of his prison shows, and soon, he wanted to do more. He told Terry Gross in 1997, "So the requests started coming in from other prisoners all over the United States. And then the word got around. So I always wanted to record that, you know, to record a show because of the reaction I got. It was far and above anything I had ever had in my life, the complete explosion of noise and reaction that they gave me with every song. So then I came back the next year and played the prison again, the New Year's Day show, came back again a third year and did the show."

Eventually he testified in front of US Congress, standing up for people who he said had been "forgotten" by society. He said, "People have got to care for prison reform to come about."

JOHNNY CASH
BORN: February 26, 1932
HOMETOWN: Kingsland, Arkansas, USA
ALBUMS SOLD: 90 million
AWARDS WON: 20 Grammy Awards

CHANCE the RAPPER

CHANCELOR BENNETT GOT SUSPENDED FROM HIS CHICAGO SCHOOL AND HE DECIDED TO DO SOMETHING PRODUCTIVE WITH HIS TIME.

He and some musical friends decided to work on a mixtape, which he eventually called *10 Day* (that's how long his suspension was) and Chance the Rapper was born. It was a big hit on the internet and fame came quickly. Luckily, Chance had the skills to back it up. The next year, he made another mixtape, *Acid Rap*, and it was even more ambitious than the first. He was soon able to tour the world and become a really big rapper.

But Chance has never stopped loving his hometown. He founded an organization called SocialWorks that aims to make Chicago a better place for kids who live there. He's also raised a ton of money for Chicago's public schools. He often hosts open mic nights that are free for college students. Some people even think he's going to run for mayor of Chicago one day.

On *What's Good with Stretch & Bobbito*, he said he started getting interested in making change when people turned him away from helping. "All the channels I was going through I just kept getting the same answers, so I said, 'I'll donate the money and see how the people respond and how the media responds, and see if anything gets fast-tracked,'" he said. "I think it's not just on artists or philanthropists to make the change; it is everybody's job to make it a conversation."

Listen to "SUNDAY CANDY." It's one of the songs that sums up who Chance is as an artist and person. The music takes cues from jazz, gospel, and R&B. Listen to the drums and the horn section. Chance often plays live with a full band of his friends behind him and you can practically feel their love on the track. On this song, Chance raps about his grandma, God, and his drive in life.

CHANCE THE RAPPER
BORN : April 16, 1993
HOMETOWN: Chicago, Illinois, USA
ESSENTIAL ALBUM: Coloring Book
AWARDS WON: 3 Grammy Awards

TAKE A STAND WITH
KESHA

KESHA STARTED OUT HER CAREER AS A TOTAL WILD CHILD.

Listen to her debut single "TIK TOK." It's a party song about going out at night and having messy fun. It's great to dance and sing along to. Her first album is filled with songs like these. Listen to "WE R WHO WE R," an encouraging song about living life as your true self and not taking "no" for an answer.

That's the kind of spiritual message Kesha believes in, and in her newer work, she has different ambitions from just singing party songs. She was raised by her mother Pebe Sebert, who was a country music songwriter, so Kesha always aspired to make music closer to the tunes she grew up with. But when she wanted to pivot, she said her label and her boss didn't want to let her. Kesha says that the people who signed her wanted to control her and were mistreating her. Along with others, including Janelle Monáe, Kesha showed her support of the *Time's Up* movement for gender equality, which addresses things like safe working environments and equal pay. After a long legal battle and a lot of time finding herself, she released an album called *Rainbow*.

But now listen to one of Kesha's more recent songs, like "PRAYING." It's different from the music that she previously released. It's hopeful and Kesha's voice soars, especially in one really high note near the end. It's not party music, but it makes you feel good in a way you wouldn't expect. It's an evolution of her sound.

KESHA
BORN: March 1, 1987
HOMETOWN: Los Angeles, California, USA
ESSENTIAL ALBUM: Rainbow
BONUS FACT: Kesha has a genius-level IQ score.

Kesha's proud of her new musical life and what it means for other artists and women who have not felt in control of their lives. In 2018, she told *Cosmopolitan*, "I've taken ownership of myself. I'm taking control of my life and my name and the music it's attached to. I would write, and pain would turn into art, and art would turn into healing, and the healing turned into a record. And then I was nominated for a Grammy!"

TAKE A STAND WITH

MS. LAURYN HILL

LAURYN HILL HAS CHANGED THE WORLD SEVERAL TIMES OVER.

As a member of the hip-hop group Fugees, she created some of the best songs of the 1990s. They were rooted in rap but worked in many different kinds of musical influences. Listen to "KILLING ME SOFTLY" from their 1996 album *The Score*. Lauryn's voice is extremely haunting but still smooth as silk. The album went on to become the best-selling hip-hop album of its time and a certified classic.

While working on some material intended for other people, Lauryn ended up with a small collection of songs and decided to craft a solo album. Being the musical genius that she is, she decided that she would produce and write the project herself. Still, after all of her success, people pushed her to work with outside artists. She resisted, and *The Miseducation of Lauryn Hill* became her crowning artistic achievement. She won five Grammy Awards, including Album of the Year. For a taste of the album's greatness, listen to "DOO WOP (THAT THING)." The song sounds like a throwback to another time but also a giant leap into the future. Lauryn is one of the greatest rappers of all time regardless of her gender, and on songs like "LOST ONES" and "FINAL HOUR," she proves this. On "EVERYTHING IS EVERYTHING" and "TO ZION," she displays that she's also one of the greatest singers ever.

Speaking about her creative control of the project to *Rock's Backpages*, Lauryn held her head up high. "Believe it or not," she said, "people still think there's some man behind the scenes, pulling the strings and manipulating what you say. And they're always looking for that person so, rather than give you the respect for having the knowledge to know what you want and do it, they're always looking for whoever that guy is who controls you. It's silly, but... whatever. It is what it is, and I don't really allow those things to stop me. I just continue, and let the music speak for itself."

MS. LAURYN HILL
BORN: *May 26, 1975*
HOMETOWN: *East Orange, New Jersey, USA*
ALBUMS SOLD: *19 million*
AWARDS WON: *8 Grammy Awards*

TAKE A STAND WITH

M.I.A.

BORN IN LONDON AND RAISED IN SRI LANKA, MATHANGI ARULPRAGASAM, BETTER KNOWN AS M.I.A., ALWAYS CONSIDERS A WORLDWIDE PERSPECTIVE WHEN SHE'S CREATING HER ART.

Her music is a complete universe without any borders. It's firmly rooted in American hip-hop, mixed with sounds from Southeast Asia, and then run through a filter of the modern internet. For a sample of what that's like, listen to "PAPER PLANES." You might know it from the hook—those cash register explosions are very striking. But pay attention to her flow in the verses. Her delivery is so casually cool and it makes the song work so well. Listen to "BOYZ" off her album *Kala* for another taste of what M.I.A. can really do. It's always good to discover sounds and rhythms you might not have heard before.

M.I.A. is fiercely political in her work. Without many Sri Lankans in the spotlight, she's taken it upon herself to be a champion for her people. As a civil war tore its way through the country, she was an outspoken activist about the situation. When she was given a medal by the Queen of England, in 2019, for her artistic achievements, she publicly noted that her mother had been the one stitching those medals for the Queen for 30 years. It was one of the only jobs her mother could get as a young refugee in London.

"It's a luxury not to be political in your work," she said to the *Atlantic* in 2018. "If I lived in the land of marshmallows with unicorns flying around, that is what my art would be about. But unfortunately, what I know is what I know. And that's what I make work about. As the only [mainstream] Tamil musician who made it to the West ever, it was not an option to remove that."

M.I.A.
BORN: July 18, 1975
HOMETOWN: London, England
ESSENTIAL ALBUM: Kala
BONUS FACT: M.I.A. is also a designer and painter.

TAKE A STAND WITH

SOLANGE

SOLANGE
BORN: *June 24, 1986*
HOMETOWN : *Houston, Texas, USA*
ESSENTIAL ALBUM: *A Seat at the Table*
AWARDS WON: *1 Grammy Award*

SOLANGE IS A TRUE ORIGINAL.

As the younger sister of Beyoncé, Solange was boxed in by some people who thought she might strike a similar path to the pop superstar. But Solange has managed to chart her own course and become a superstar in her own right. Listening to Solange is like sitting through an art and philosophy course that also somehow happens to be the chillest dance party you could ever imagine.

Listen to "DON'T TOUCH MY HAIR." It's a song about the ways people casually violate the singer, her protected spaces, and her whole race in general. It might be shocking to some, but it's vital to listen to messages with open ears and an open mind. It's a fresh-sounding piece of music and Solange wouldn't have made it without completely believing in herself as an artist.

In an interview with older sister Beyoncé for *Interview* magazine, she spoke about what drives her creative process. "I remember being really young and having this voice inside that told me to trust my gut," she said. "And my gut has been really, really strong in my life. It's pretty vocal and it leads me. Sometimes I haven't listened, and those times didn't end up very well for me." That gut makes some wild choices. Listen to "LOSING YOU." It sounds like sprinting through a carnival in a completely different galaxy. The percussion throughout the song is wonderous and Solange's voice shines through like a sunbeam. Now listen to "CRANES IN THE SKY." It's from her 2016 album, called *A Seat at the Table*, which is a profound collection of songs about her identity as a Black woman and her family's history. This song in particular is a special moment where Solange unpacks the experience of dealing with grief. At points her voice sounds like it's going to break, but then it rises straight up to the ceiling. It's incredibly moving.

WHEN YOU'RE FEELING
ALL CHARGED UP AND READY
TO GO,

RELEASE ENERGY WITH...

RELEASE ENERGY WITH

Blondie

BLONDIE
*HOMETOWN: New York,
New York, USA*
ALBUMS SOLD: 40 million
ESSENTIAL ALBUM: Parallel Lines
*AWARDS WON: 1 Grammy Hall of
Fame Award*

DEBBIE HARRY AND THE OTHER MEMBERS OF BLONDIE ARE LIKE A BIG VACUUM: THEY SUCK UP ALL OF THE MUSIC THAT'S GOING ON AROUND THEM, LETTING IT ALL SIT TOGETHER AND TURNING INTO A BIG HAPPY MESS.

Listen to "RAPTURE." Released in 1980, it represents everything that was going on around them in New York City at the time: you can hear disco, new wave, punk, and hip-hop influences on the track. It's all carried through by a funky bass and Debbie Harry's deadpan voice. In the middle of the song, Debbie raps a verse. For a lot of people all over the world, this was the first rap song they fell in love with. In the verse, she tips her hat to her friend, rap pioneer Fab Five Freddy, and throughout her career she has been quick to credit his impact on her, as well as all of the people she's learned from. It's always important to acknowledge originators when you're taking the energy around you and turning it into something else.

The band has always harnessed that energy well, starting out in downtown clubs like NYC's famous CBGB, and it still tours and makes new music today. Listening to Blondie makes you feel like you're discovering something great from the underground.

But being a genre-defying, New York City great means that your loved ones might not always understand you. Debbie Harry, told *VICE* magazine that her parents always wanted her to become a "housewife and mother." She chose rock star. "They did not want me to venture forth—they wanted me to stay right there," she said. "They never really accepted my career... They would always have preferred me to lead a 'normal' life. I mean, they were very old-fashioned. I think they were proud, but it was all so foreign to them that they wondered who I was... as I wondered who they were."

RELEASE ENERGY WITH

NO DOUBT

LISTEN TO "I'M JUST A GIRL" BY CALIFORNIA ROCK BAND NO DOUBT.

The second that dramatic guitar riff begins, you know they're going to have something to say. Then singer Gwen Stefani starts to sing about her frustrations with being treated like a fragile piece of china and you're all ears. When the band sings their "whoas" behind her, there's no way to resist the song at all.

Writing the song, as Gwen recounted, in an interview with *People* magazine, was an unforgettable experience. "My parents were quite strict with me and I was living at home, even into my twenties. And I would have to come home and knock on my parents' door. And it was frustrating because I was already, like, older," Stefani said. "I can remember thinking, 'Wow, I'm in the car right now, I'm driving home, it's like one in the morning and if something did happen to me, I'm vulnerable because I'm a girl.' And you start to think, 'Wow, maybe people actually look at me different because I am a female.'"

"I'm Just a Girl" was part of the band's breakthrough album *Tragic Kingdom*, which came out in 1995. The album masterfully takes the chill sounds of ska, and blends them with punk and pop elements. Listen to "SPIDERWEBS," another example of how they blend musical genres. You've got a bunch of horns that lead the song, and then a super funky bass picks up where they left off as Gwen sings about dodging phone calls from someone she wants to forget.

Most of the lyrics on the album were written by Gwen about her breakup with the band's bassist Tony Kanal. (For the most brutal of those songs, listen to "DON'T SPEAK"—it just might break your heart a little bit.) It's a case of taking extremely negative energy and putting it back into the universe as creative brilliance. The two are still friendly to this day, and created tons of successful music together.

NO DOUBT
HOMETOWN : Anaheim, California, USA
ESSENTIAL ALBUM: Tragic Kingdom
AWARDS WON: 2 Grammy Awards
BONUS FACT: The band originally had a whole horn section.

82

RELEASE ENERGY WITH

blur

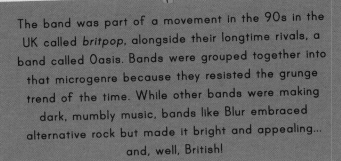

LISTEN TO "SONG 2." THE CHEEKILY TITLED SONG IS LIKE A SOUND EXPLOSION IN YOUR HEADPHONES.

When Damon Albarn "woo-hoos" into your ears, you want to scream along with him. Listening to Blur sometimes sounds like getting thrown out of an airplane at 20,000 feet with a giant smile on your face.

The band was part of a movement in the 90s in the UK called *britpop*, alongside their longtime rivals, a band called Oasis. Bands were grouped together into that microgenre because they resisted the grunge trend of the time. While other bands were making dark, mumbly music, bands like Blur embraced alternative rock but made it bright and appealing... and, well, British!

After a string of hits, the band broke up in 2003. Lead singer Damon Albarn went on to create another band called Gorillaz, which was extremely successful. Listen to their song "FEEL GOOD INC." for a taste of what they're all about.

Eventually the members of Blur made amends and made another record together in 2015 after taking a trip together. Reflecting on the breakup years later, guitarist Graham Coxon told *Rolling Stone* that it happened because he was quite selfish at the time. "Young men are volatile, weird creatures, especially when they're tired of being told a bunch of stuff they don't really want to do. We were all going through the same thing, but they were probably just a little more professional than I was. I wanted to make amends to the fans and the group after all that trouble I caused years ago."

Their reformation is a reminder that you can always work on fixing things. (Eventually Albarn made some music with a member of Oasis.) Getting rid of your own negative energy is a pivotal step in growing up.

BLUR
HOMETOWN: Sheffield, England
ESSENTIAL ALBUM: Parklife
BONUS FACT: The milk cartons in their video for "Coffee and TV" were made by Jim Henson's Creature Shop.
AWARDS WON: BRIT Award for Outstanding Contribution to Music

RELEASE ENERGY WITH

SLEATER-KINNEY

ROCK MUSIC IN THE 90S WAS LARGELY DOMINATED BY MEN.

But Sleater-Kinney proved that women could be just as hardcore as any guy. Carrie Brownstein, Corin Tucker, and Janet Weiss made some of the most passionate guitar music of the decade, and built one of the strongest communities around them in the process.

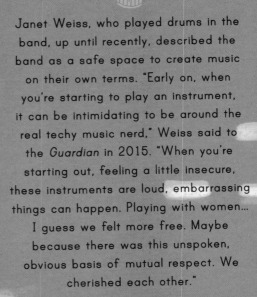

Janet Weiss, who played drums in the band, up until recently, described the band as a safe space to create music on their own terms. "Early on, when you're starting to play an instrument, it can be intimidating to be around the real techy music nerd," Weiss said to the *Guardian* in 2015. "When you're starting out, feeling a little insecure, these instruments are loud, embarrassing things can happen. Playing with women... I guess we felt more free. Maybe because there was this unspoken, obvious basis of mutual respect. We cherished each other."

They are the founding members of the riot grrrl scene that helped women define and declare themselves through punk style, music, and attitude. Sleater-Kinney's music encourages listeners to be themselves, stand up to bullies, and do whatever it is that they want to do. They're a band that built support around themselves without breaking sales records or taking over the radio. They did all that through the power of song and the political message behind their work.

Their loving energy mixed with the raw aggression in their songs is what makes Sleater-Kinney so special. Listening to their music is like smashing some old junk with a sledgehammer. Try out "DIG ME OUT" from their 1997 album of the same name. Pay attention to how the two guitars play off each other, in turns complementing and competing with each other. For a more polished but still blistering take from them, try "A NEW WAVE." They're still tense as ever, but there's a renewed focus to the music that makes it feel even more important.

SLEATER-KINNEY
HOMETOWN: Olympia, Washington, USA
BONUS FACT: Singer Carrie Brownstein has also done comedy acting and writing.
ESSENTIAL ALBUM: The Woods
ALBUMS SOLD: 1 million

RELEASE ENERGY WITH → THE PIXIES

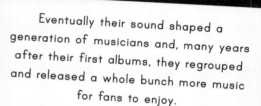

THE PIXIES
HOMETOWN: *Boston, Massachusetts*
ALBUMS SOLD: *1 million*
ESSENTIAL ALBUM: *Doolittle*
BONUS FACT: *The band found its first major inspiration in Puerto Rico.*

THE PIXIES CAME OUT OF BOSTON IN THE EARLY 90S AND WEREN'T A BREAKAWAY SUCCESS OUT OF THE GATE.

Their music actually didn't catch on for the most part until they broke up. But a bunch of bands were inspired by their weird lyrics and the unique way they structured their songs. They're famous for making songs that play with the balance between loud and quiet.

To experience that phenomenon, listen to "GIGANTIC." It starts off with a bassline thump as Frank Black howls off in the distance. Singer Kim Deal comes in after this, singing softly. Then the chorus hits like an explosion. The whole band—guitar, bass, drums, and multiple vocalists—comes to life, and it's a huge celebration. That's the magic of listening to the Pixies: there's always an unexpected twist just around the corner. It's about controlling and conserving energy and then letting it all hang out.

Eventually their sound shaped a generation of musicians and, many years after their first albums, they regrouped and released a whole bunch more music for fans to enjoy.

Creating those songs, Black says, was an exercise in letting go completely. In order to create, he had to escape his worries and judgements. "I just didn't question anything," Black affirmed. "I didn't question the lyrics or the sound. I didn't try to present any particular angle or philosophy; it wasn't about trying to represent our generation. It was more escapist and art-gallery. Making pretty pictures, or ugly pictures, and framing them. It was high art."

Listen to "WHERE IS MY MIND?" probably their best-known song. It features Black on lead vocals and again plays with quiet and loud noises in interesting ways. The whistling howl that guides the song is instantly unforgettable. In the chorus, it's just Frank and the drums letting you relax, until everything comes back in and a second part of the story can begin, guitars ablaze.

RELEASE ENERGY WITH

Arctic Monkeys

WATCH THE VIDEO FOR "DO I WANNA KNOW?" BY ARCTIC MONKEYS.

It starts off with just a sound wave, transforming as the band's guitar pumps through your speakers. But slowly the ordinary music turns into something different, and so do the animations. Boots stomp down, cars fly by, and bodies morph out of the ether as the band takes a regular rock song into new, weirder territory.

ARCTIC MONKEYS
HOMETOWN: Sheffield, England
ESSENTIAL ALBUM: AM
AWARDS WON: 7 BRIT Awards
BONUS FACT: The band became popular on early social media site, MySpace.

That's what Arctic Monkeys are all about, taking the ordinary and making it cooler and more alien. Listen to "I BET YOU LOOK GOOD ON THE DANCEFLOOR," a three-minute song that's as fast as a Formula One race car. The guitars and the drums sound like they're fighting—in a good way!—as Alex Turner screams over them.

The band made early gains in popularity through the internet, which seems like an obvious sort of thing now, but at the time was very revolutionary. They gained fans from all over the world by giving away their songs for free online.

Part of the band's pull is its oddball lyrics and Sheffield charm. Most lyrics are written by Turner. Some of them weirdly sound closer to out-there rap lyrics than traditional rock lyrics. Writing songs with that much energy is something he's been doing since his school days. When asked about it, he says that it comes down to commitment. "If anyone asks me about songwriting, I guess I'd say that you just gotta do it. I remember being afraid almost, to write [stuff] down," he said. "It's just about practice; you get better."

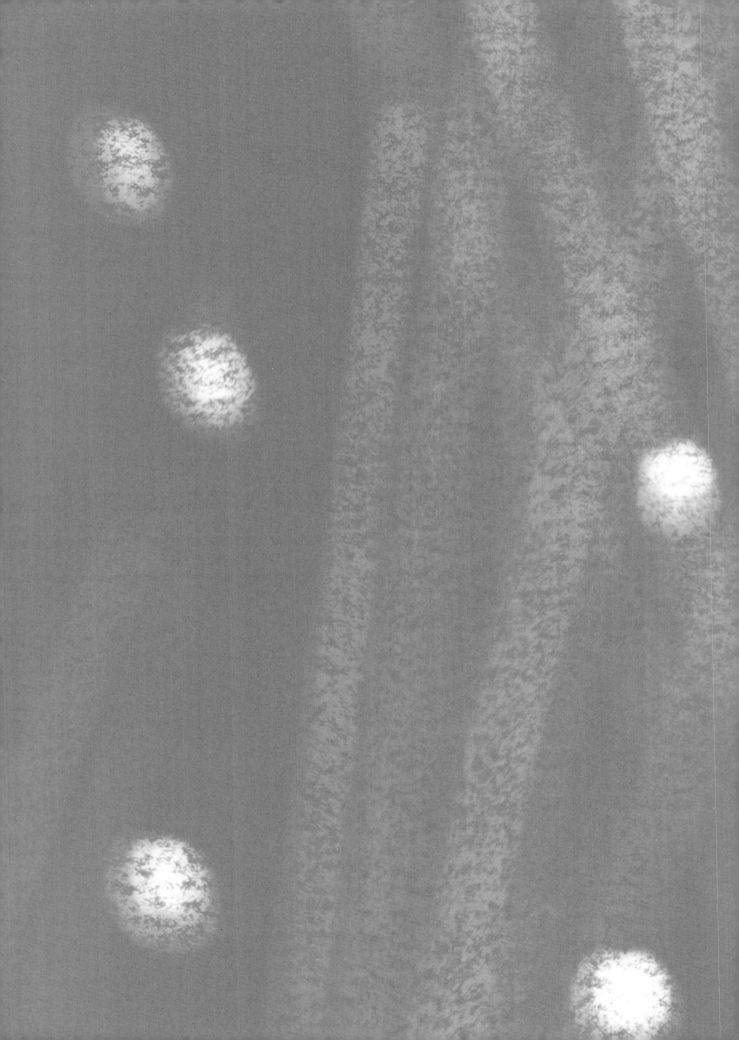

WHEN YOU'RE ANGRY,
AGGRIEVED, IRRITATED, OR
EXASPERATED,

SHOUT ABOUT IT WITH...

SHOUT ABOUT IT WITH
ALANIS MORISSETTE

ALANIS MORISSETTE QUIETLY STEPPED OUT OF CANADA AND CHANGED THE WORLD.

In 1994 she moved from Toronto to Los Angeles after releasing two albums that received local love but failed to attract a broader audience. She buckled down in a studio and crafted an album, eventually called *Jagged Little Pill*, that was so forthcoming and so cool that no one in the world could deny her talent.

Years later, Alanis reflected on writing those songs. "There is this illusion of safety for artists, when you're alone in a room," she said. "Until the crazy fame that ensued, I literally thought maybe 10 people would hear this song. I didn't think anyone would really hear it. I mean, I wanted to share it with as many billions of people as I possibly could, but I was alone in a room with [my producer], and it was safe for me to talk and share and write, and so I did, and it felt really liberating. It was only later that I realized that my own personal intimate experiences were things that people related to or were inspired by or comforted by."

People sought refuge in Alanis's lyrics. Listen to "YOU OUGHTA KNOW." It's the song that launched her career into the stratosphere. Over the funkiest bass line possible, Alanis lets out a vicious scream about a man who treated her poorly. That same booming voice is present on a lighter song like "IRONIC" too. But the album has a much softer side. Listen to "HAND IN MY POCKET," where Alanis defines herself to her listeners. You might just find something in common with her and find yourself singing along.

Listening to Alanis Morissette is understanding that sometimes the world might be a little harsh but it's all going to be all right as long as you work to keep your head on straight.

ALANIS MORISSETTE
BORN: June 1, 1974
HOMETOWN: Ottawa, Ontario, Canada
ALBUMS SOLD: 75 million
AWARDS WON: 7 Grammy Awards

SHOUT ABOUT IT WITH

PARAMORE

PARAMORE
HOMETOWN: Franklin, Tennessee, USA
ESSENTIAL ALBUM: Riot!
BONUS FACT: Paramore puts together an annual vacation, called Parahoy!, with their fans on a cruise ship.
AWARDS WON: 1 Grammy Award

13-YEAR-OLD HAYLEY WILLIAMS HAD SOMETHING TO SAY.

The teen singer met up with Josh and Zac Farro and some other like-minded teens in her hometown, and formed a group called Paramore who gave her the backing and push she needed to step up to the microphone.

Still, Hayley had some doubts about seeing herself in the lead role. "I doubted whether people would ever take me seriously," she said. "I felt like I needed to be part of a boys' club to make it... It really affected my sense of self and what I thought I owed people. I thought I had to be better than them to prove my worth. I wish I'd learned sooner that [being a woman] is actually this incredible strength."

But her songs were undeniable. Listen to "MISERY BUSINESS" to start off. The guitars are lightning fast and the drums might make your head thump. Hayley's delivery keeps time with the guitars and then breaks into the extraordinary chorus—her "Whoaaa's" are perfect ear candy that wake you up inside. There's just something about the way Hayley writes her songs that connects with people. Listening to Paramore is like telling an understanding friend your big secrets and then throwing a giant party to celebrate how free you feel.

As the band grew up, so did their music. "AIN'T IT FUN" is one of their best songs. Hayley's voice still has a similar tenacity like her early songs, but you can tell that she's found a greater source of inner power to draw from. That chorus is still loud as anything, but pay attention to what happens toward the middle of the song: a whole chorus joins behind her to amplify her voice and sing along.

Hayley Williams redefined what it meant to be a rock star in her time. People of any gender can appreciate how hard she had to work to get to the top of her game, how much practice it took, and how much commitment to writing honest lyrics.

SHOUT ABOUT IT WITH

RADIOHEAD

RADIOHEAD IS FURTHER PROOF THAT BEING A WEIRDO PAYS OFF.

The band is made up of lead singer and multi-instrumentalist Thom Yorke, guitarist Jonny Greenwood, bass player Colin Greenwood, drummer Philip Selway, and guitarist Ed O'Brien, who contributes a lot of extra sounds. That last description might not make sense if you've never listened to Radiohead before, but will make perfect sense once you do.

In the spirit of Radiohead, start out with one of their freakier songs: specifically "15 STEP" from their 2007 album *In Rainbows*. It starts off with scattered noises and then seamlessly blends into strummed guitar music. Thom Yorke's voice blends into whatever music necessary. Sometimes those noises pop out of nowhere and they can be like screams of aliens.

The recording process can be an odd one for a band like Radiohead. In an interview with *Guitar World*, Thom Yorke described how "KARMA POLICE" was composed. "We said, 'Put down the headphones and just go,'" said Yorke, "and so [Ed] made weird noises, and we taped that a few times. Sometimes the best stuff happens when you're not even listening at all. Once we get to a studio, we either do it together live at the same time, so we can hear what we're doing, or we do the exact opposite, so we don't know what's going on at all. There's no middle ground."

But the band has more straightforward hits in their catalog as well. Listen to "KARMA POLICE." It's a spine-tingling ballad sung over piano but at times it can sound like Thom Yorke is a wolf howling at the moon. Then, at the end, everything goes fuzzy and those extraterrestrial sounds come in again. Listening to Radiohead is always a surprise, but you walk away from it learning something new about music and maybe yourself, your politics, or your emotions.

RADIOHEAD
HOMETOWN: Abingdon-on-Thames, England
ALBUMS SOLD: 30 million
AWARDS WON: 6 Grammy Awards
ESSENTIAL ALBUM: OK Computer

SHOUT ABOUT IT WITH

NIRVANA

NIRVANA
HOMETOWN: Seattle, Washington, USA
ALBUMS SOLD: 100 million
AWARDS WON: Rock and Roll Hall of Fame
ESSENTIAL ALBUM: Nevermind

TO GET TO KNOW NIRVANA, YOU SHOULD LISTEN TO THE SONG THAT INTRODUCED THEM TO MOST OF THE WORLD.

"SMELLS LIKE TEEN SPIRIT" was a song that defined a generation. It's kind of creepy-sounding and the band's lead singer, Kurt Cobain, barely sings above a groan until the chorus hits, and then he's screaming with insane intensity. It makes you want to get out of your seat and scream along. That's what listening to Nirvana does for their fans: they find comfort in sharing some screams.

Kurt, alongside bassist Krist Novoselic and drummer Dave Grohl, released lots of songs as loud and powerful as "SMELLS LIKE TEEN SPIRIT." (Their masterpiece, *Nevermind*, is a good place to start.) But it wasn't their volume that hooked millions of fans to their music—it was the emotion behind the yelling. See if you can find a video of their 1994 acoustic performance for *MTV Unplugged*. For many people, that concert was a turning point in how they understood the band: not just as angry musicians, but as incredible artists. In the middle of the special, they play a cover of David Bowie's "THE MAN WHO SOLD THE WORLD." Kurt barely has to raise his voice to get any of his feelings across.

Kurt led a troubled life but the one thing he was committed to more than anything was making music and writing out his feelings. "While there's a certain selfish gratification in having any number of people buy your records and come to see you play," Kurt said, "none of that holds a candle to simply hearing a song that I've written played by a band. I'm not talking about radio or MTV. I just really like playing these songs with a good drummer and bass player. Next to my wife and daughter, there's nothing that brings me more pleasure."

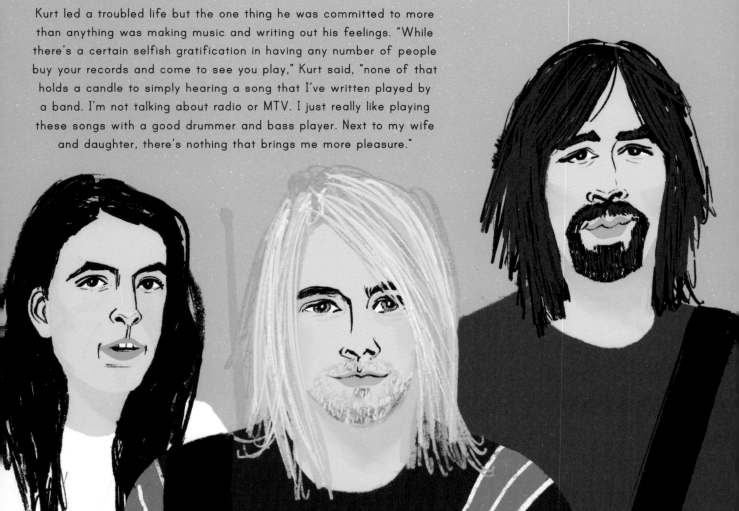

WHEN YOU'VE JUST GOT TO
MOVE YOUR BODY TO THE BEAT,

DANCE AROUND WITH...

DANCE AROUND WITH

BRUNO MARS

BRUNO MARS WANTS TO MAKE YOU FALL IN LOVE WITH HIS SONGS.

Or at least for everyone to have a good time. Start with "THAT'S WHAT I LIKE," where he croons so sweetly to his love over a springy beat. It's the latest in his long line of hits that can make someone of any age feel warm inside.

BRUNO MARS
BORN: October 8, 1985
HOMETOWN: Honolulu, Hawai'i, USA
ALBUMS SOLD: 26 million
AWARDS WON: 11 Grammy Awards;
3 BRIT Awards

He got his start as a performer doing covers of Elvis Presley around Hawai'i. Eventually he became a songwriter in Hollywood and then transitioned into making his own music. He's probably best known for "UPTOWN FUNK," a song he released in 2014 with the producer Mark Ronson. It took over the world when it was released. Listening to Bruno Mars is like being at your best friend's wedding: you're going to dance, celebrate the special people in your life, and maybe fall in love yourself.

Bruno summarized his intense feelings about the connection between music, love, and dancing to NME.

"For me, 95 percent of music is about love," he said. "...Get people on the dance floor, get the girls smiling. That was my childhood; that's why I fell in love with music. Those 90s songs are what I was singing to get the girls in school, the songs that the girls like, what we were dancing to as children... I think the the reason why that music resonates so much for me is that it made it okay to dance – it was cool to dance. It was cool to fall in love and smile and flirt on the dance floor."

DANCE AROUND WITH

ABBA

SEE IF YOU CAN FIND FOOTAGE OF SWEDISH BAND ABBA COMPETING IN *EUROVISION* IN 1974.

Agnetha Fältskog and Anni-Frid Lyngstad run onto the stage in the most 1970s outfits imaginable—lots of jewel tones and big, big hair. But the song that they belt out, alongside their bandmates Benny Andersson and Björn Ulvaeus, is kind of stunning, if a little earnest. It's called "WATERLOO," and it's quintessential ABBA (their band names comes from the mashup of Agnetha, Benny, Björn, and Anni-Frid). Even if you don't really enjoy the song it will be looping around in your head for the next few days (or even years).

ABBA
HOMETOWN: Stockholm, Sweden
ALBUMS SOLD: 50 million
ESSENTIAL ALBUM: Waterloo
BONUS FACT: Mamma Mia, a Broadway musical featuring their hit songs, has been turned into two movies.

105

They went on to win the competition that year, a success story that rocketed them to international fame. Throughout their career, they made songs that were pure ear candy from start to finish without any exceptions.

But even with their extreme songwriting chops, they were extremely humble about the longevity of their careers. "We didn't think the music would live on this long," Benny said. "You know what pop music is. It is there for the time it actually happens. You are on the charts for sixteen weeks or four weeks, then it goes and then something else comes up. Another band comes in. Another trend comes in. You think that's the way it should be. We were absolutely dead sure that it would be the same for us."

Listen to "DANCING QUEEN." There's something about it that makes you take off your cool and dance around without a care.

DANCE AROUND WITH

DIANA ROSS

TWO OF THE BEST DANCE SONGS OF ALL TIME WERE CREATED FROM THE SAME SENTENCE.

When the ultimate diva Diana Ross met superstar producer Nile Rodgers before working together on her 1980 album *Diana*, they didn't know what they were going to make. After transforming motown with the Supremes and experiencing success in a solo career, Diana Ross was at a bit of a crossroads in her career. The producer asked her a simple question: "What do you want to sing about?" She replied, "I don't know. I'm just coming out and everything's upside down." And so the two of them spearheaded the creation of "UPSIDE DOWN" and "I'M COMING OUT."

Listen to the first of those songs. The groove is incredible, and Diana matches it beat for beat. You can practically hear her smiling as she's singing. The same can be said for "I'm Coming Out." The song has been an anthem for people seeking personal freedom since it came out, and it's easy to see why. As Diana sings about liberating herself, the feeling is contagious. Listening to the song makes your whole being feel lighter. That's the power of Diana Ross: she brings a measure of humanity to her music that cannot be imitated or reproduced. That honesty is a singular talent that has given her one of the most storied careers in pop music.

For Diana Ross, music just flows out of her naturally, like breathing. "I sing all the time. Music is a part of my being," she said. "Like when I'm walking, I walk with a rhythm. I carry myself as if there's music inside. I can be on an elevator and I might hum a song or sing something, and someone might get off the elevator and say, 'Thanks for this concert.' And I don't even realize I'm humming."

DIANA ROSS
BORN: March 26, 1944
HOMETOWN: Detroit, Michigan, USA
ALBUMS SOLD: 71 million
AWARDS WON: 1 Grammy Award

QUEEN

THERE'S NEVER BEEN A BAND LIKE QUEEN.

Fronted by mythical singer Freddie Mercury, they created a collection of songs that seem like fairy tales sent to Earth from very far-off galaxies.

For an easy introduction to the band, listen to "DON'T STOP ME NOW." It begins with just Freddie and some piano accompanying him, like he's a ringmaster introducing you to his circus. Then the song builds gigantically from there. All of a sudden, there are shredding electric guitars, a kicking drumbeat, and a full choir or two thrown in there for good luck. It's pure excess, and something that gets you out of your seat right away.

Freddie Mercury spoke freely about the way real-life emotions impacted his music. He was someone who effectively captured his feelings in song. "I'm possessed by love — but isn't everybody?," he once asked an interview. "Most of my songs are love ballads and things to do with sadness and torture and pain. In terms of love you're not in control and I hate that feeling. seem to write a lot of sad songs because I'm a very tragic person. But there's always an element of humour at the er

QUEEN
HOMETOWN : *London, Eng*
ALBUMS SOLD : *300 milli*
AWARDS WON : *Rock and
Hall of Fame*
ESSENTIAL ALBUM: *News
the World*

All of those emotions and more are on display in the band's song "BOHEMIAN RHAPSODY." The song is somehow only six minutes long but contains a lifetime of stories and moods. Freddie started writing it in the late 60s and didn't end up recording it until almost a decade later. It was really three songs he made up, combined into a mini opera. The rest of the band went along with his daring plan and had a ball doing it. There are parts to sway along to, parts to bang your head to, and parts to jump up and down to. It's a masterpiece of music to enjoy.

108

DANCE AROUND WITH

MADONNA

MADONNA'S LIFE STORY IS TOLD BEST WHEN IT'S DONE BY MADONNA HERSELF.

"I went to New York," she said in her 1985 documentary. "I had a dream. I wanted to be a big star. I didn't know anybody. I wanted to dance. I wanted to sing... I wanted to make people happy. I wanted to be famous. I wanted everybody to love me. I wanted to be a star. I worked really hard and my dream came true."

MADONNA
BORN: August 16, 1958
HOMETOWN : Bay City,
Michigan, USA
ALBUMS SOLD: 300 million
AWARDS WON : 7 Grammy Awards

From the release of her first single "EVERYBODY" in 1982, Madonna knew how to get people talking with her mix of wondrous dance music and crazy fashions. She's courted controversy throughout her career as the "Queen of Pop," but her heart has always been in the right place. As an artist and woman, she stands for not following the rules and letting people be as free as they want to be. Her music is of a similar nature.

Listen to "LIKE A PRAYER." It takes elements from gospel, rock, and pop, and turns them into something wholly original. Listening to Madonna's music is always thrilling. One minute you might find yourself ready to cry and you'll be screaming and dancing along with her before you even realize what happened.

Madonna's whole catalog is jam-packed with songs you should dance to. From early hits like "HOLIDAY" and "INTO THE GROOVE," to later jams like "4 MINUTES," there's a Madonna song for every occasion. Listen to "HUNG UP," from her 2005 album *Confessions on a Dance Floor*. The album is a tribute to her early years in New York City's club scene. For something completely different, listen to "RAY OF LIGHT." It's from an album of the same name that many critics consider to be her best work. It shows a more thoughtful side of her that might make you dance too.

DANCE AROUND WITH

ROBYN

ROBYN CREATES MUSIC FOR DANCING OUT YOUR PROBLEMS.

For the most shining example, listen to "DANCING ON MY OWN." The opening synth noises will make you feel like you're in the center of a disco ball. But almost immediately, Robyn cuts through it all with some heart-shattering lyrics about hearing that someone she loves is with someone new. By the chorus, she's taking you on her journey of watching them be happy together, an experience that's never enjoyable.

But the song is true to life: just because you're out having fun, doesn't mean that all your problems go away. But by listening to Robyn, you understand that there's someone out there going through the same stuff that you are.

In an interview with the *New York Times*, Robyn spoke about the way dance music unlocked an essential part of herself. "Club music taught me so much about myself," she said. "[Like] having patience, or appreciating a different type of way of taking in life. It's a hypnotic thing. Time stops, and I don't even think about where I am when I hear music like that. That's the high that I want. That's what I need."

Sometimes you just need to try to dance it all out. For those occasions, there's Robyn. If you get tired of "DANCING ON MY OWN" after too many plays, you can play "CALL YOUR GIRLFRIEND" or "HANG WITH ME."

Robyn doesn't just deal in heartbreak though. Try listening "INDESTRUCTIBLE," "HONEY," or "EVER AGAIN" to get three completely different sides of the Swedish singer. On the first one, she's projecting strength to a magnificent degree—try and match her if you can. On the second, she's warm and lovable. On the last one, she's practically spinning around in circles. Like all great songwriters, Robyn manages to capture the best of what it is to be human.

ROBYN
BORN: 12 June 1979
HOMETOWN:
Stockholm, Sweden
ESSENTIAL ALBUM:
Body Talk
BONUS FACT: Robyn signed her first recording contract when she was 14 years old.

A FINAL NOTE...

There's no wrong way to listen to any of these artists. Plug in your headphones and enjoy a quiet moment with your favorite storytellers, blast your favorite songs on speakers and dance around, or go see some artists play their music live. With each way—and many more!— you'll find new experiences to enjoy the soundtrack to your life.

It shouldn't stop at just audio, too. Watch music videos and old performances online. Get a sense of how artists blend their music with visual styles and fashion to create an entire persona. For lots of artists here, the statements they've made with their videos and their looks have been as important to their careers as any albums.

No matter which way you consume music, don't be afraid to go deep with your connection to what you're hearing. Let music help you out when you're not at the top of your game. Elton John once said, "Music has healing power. It has the ability to take people out of themselves for a few hours." Embrace that, and let your favorite songs be your escape from the world.

A lot of artists feel restored by people finding refuge in their songs. The relationship that they have with their fans fuels their creative processes. Lady Gaga has a close personal relationship with her fans and she says that's what keeps her going. "When I see or hear from them that the music that I've made has changed their life in some way, that's what makes me feel beautiful," she said. "At the end of the day, I could be in a million movies and put out a million songs and everyone could say, 'She was so beautiful,' but that's not really what I want. I want them to say, 'I saw that movie and I cried my eyes out and I learned something about myself.'"

This book is just the beginning of your journey with music! Once you find artists you like, figure out which musicians and bands they look up to. What kind of genres or sounds do they pull from to make their own music? What life events led them to write their most personal lyrics? What about their upbringing made them the kind of musicians that they are? Which producers or songwriters helped